# THE
# ECONOMICS OF
# INTEGRITY

· · · · · · · · · · · · · · · · · · · · · · ·

# THE

# ECONOMICS OF

# INTEGRITY

· · · · · · · · · · · · · · · · · · · · · · · · · · · ·

*From Dairy Farmers to Toyota,
How Wealth Is Built on Trust and
What That Means for Our Future*

· · · · · · · · · · · · · · · · · · · · · · · · · · · ·

# ANNA BERNASEK

**harper**studio
*An Imprint of* HarperCollins*Publishers*

HarperCollins books may be purchased for educational, business, or sales promotional use. For information please write: Special Markets Department, HarperCollins Publishers, 10 East 53rd Street, New York, NY 10022.

To book Anna Bernasek for a speaking engagement, visit www.harpercollinsspeakers.com.

For more information about this book or other books from HarperStudio, visit www.theharperstudio.com.

FIRST EDITION

*Designed by Joy O'Meara*

Library of Congress Cataloging-in-Publication Data

Bernasek, Anna.
    The economics of integrity : from dairy farmers to Toyota, how wealth is built on trust and what that means for our future / by Anna Bernasek.—1st ed.
        p. cm.
Includes bibliographical references.
ISBN 978-0-06-177413-3
1. Trust.   2. Integrity.   3. Economic development.   I. Title.
    BJ1500.T78B47 2010
    330.1'6—dc22
                                                            2009043097

10  11  12  13  14   DIX/RRD   10 9 8 7 6 5 4 3 2 1

*For DTM*

# CONTENTS

......................................

*Introduction: Why Integrity?*                    1

CHAPTER 1    A New Way of Thinking              5

CHAPTER 2    It's in the Milk                  17

CHAPTER 3    Behind the ATM Screen            38

CHAPTER 4    Good as Gold                     57

CHAPTER 5    Trusted Brands                   77

CHAPTER 6    Trusting Customers               95

CHAPTER 7    Trading on Your Word            112

CHAPTER 8    Lessons from a Start-Up         127

CHAPTER 9    The DNA of Integrity            146

CHAPTER 10   The Future of Integrity         168

*Acknowledgments*                           187

*Sources*                                   189

# THE
# ECONOMICS OF
# INTEGRITY

INTRODUCTION

# Why Integrity?

· · · · · · · · · · · · · · · · · · · · · · · · · · ·

At first, when I thought about the 2008 financial crisis, I was angry and pessimistic. It was by far the biggest economic disruption of my lifetime. As a nation, we've spent trillions of dollars to clean up the mess—a staggering amount of money. The effects will haunt us for decades. Beginning with those terrible concerns, I craved a way to go forward. This book is my own response to the question: What do we do now?

I have had the privilege of seeing the United States as an outsider. I was born in Boston but grew up in Australia. My father, a native of Czechoslovakia, risked his life to escape from communism in 1949 and gained political asylum in Australia. After marrying, he moved to the United States, where he earned a Ph.D. in economics and began his academic career. Like so many of his generation, my father admired the great qualities of the United States and he passed on that admiration to me.

This book pays tribute to the spirit of this nation: a spirit of optimism and idealism. America is a place where people can dream and achieve. To be true to that spirit, my focus isn't on what went wrong. I am not primarily concerned with scandals, fraud, and cheating. Instead, I examine what makes this economy great and show how we can do more of those things.

For too long, the economics profession has minimized the critical role of cooperation in economic activity. Emphasis on the individual has risen above all else and overshadowed the profound ways we depend on each other. You may have heard a successful businessperson boast, "I did it all myself." I want to interrupt at that point. Every successful business requires the cooperative effort of many people—the banker who believes in the business plan, the customer who trusts the product, the employee who devotes precious time to the business and its owners.

If we ignore the important ways people cooperate to create wealth, we miss the most valuable source of wealth creation imaginable. Recognizing the true value of relationships, we can build stronger relationships and create and share greater wealth. It's a powerful way to reinvigorate the economy.

In this era, when so much seems to be going wrong, many have lost trust in their fellow citizens. But the path forward can't be to stop trusting. We need to build the trust that will power the economy for decades to come. The purpose of this book is to show how that can be done.

I wrote this book for everyone: individuals trying to make sense of the world, companies striving to grow and make a profit, and policy makers seeking ways to build a strong future. It's my sincerest hope to inspire everyone who reads this book to see the true miracle of integrity and trust in the economy.

The economy isn't some dirty game where all the players are only out for themselves, trying to make their names and their fortunes. It's a noble project. Each one of us has a meaningful role to play. In the end, what you do really does matter.

For companies slogging it out and for those starting new business projects, I wanted to provide a picture of what really drives business. By appreciating integrity as an asset that is valuable, companies can learn how to invest in it and create wealth. Knowing the techniques for investing in integrity, brands, feedback, and communications, among other things, we can build sustainable and valuable businesses.

All too frequently we are given the false choice between free markets or regulation. It's a pointless debate that has disturbed me for some time. This book bridges the gap between left and right and provides a fundamental approach. Understanding integrity will let us have an honest debate about how to make our system better.

This book provides a tool kit for creating more integrity anywhere in the economy. When policy makers are thinking about changing health care, reforming the tax system, or improving the financial system, they can use these tools to systematically build value. I encourage readers to see that integrity unlocks enormous opportunities for wealth creation that we may not yet imagine.

CHAPTER ONE

# A New Way of Thinking

. . . . . . . . . . . . . . . . . . . . . . . . . . . . .

O n a bitter cold Monday morning in winter, Ben Bernanke, chairman of the Federal Reserve, was in his office, glued to his computer screen. The bank was eerily quiet. Government offices were closed for a national holiday, and Bernanke had canceled travel plans to be at his desk. For months, financial markets around the world had been jittery about the unfolding subprime crisis, but in the early hours of January 21, 2008, nervousness turned to outright panic. Stock markets in Asia and Europe were in free fall. Suddenly global investors were questioning whether the U.S. financial system might be on the brink of collapse.

Investors could sense a meltdown, as one major financial player after another came forward to reveal enormous losses. And there seemed to be no end in sight. If a bank as big as Citibank might not be able to pay its bills, then could anyone? Might the whole grand system of money and markets around the world grind to a terrifying halt?

For some time, Bernanke and others inside the bank had

been seeing the cracks appear. It was becoming obvious that the financial system couldn't withstand a significant shock without help from the government. Trillions of dollars, a huge share of the entire economy, had been funneled into housing-related assets. And now those massive investments were becoming increasingly shaky as the housing market reversed course. It wouldn't take much—a shock from global stock markets, for instance—and everything could start to unravel.

With the U.S. stock market set to open the next day, Bernanke made up his mind to act. He knew the arguments of his detractors. The next Open Market Committee meeting was only eight days away. Couldn't a decision wait until then? Too hasty an action could cause a loss of confidence, or even panic. But in eight days' time, Bernanke feared it might be too late.

The next day, an hour before the opening bell, the Federal Reserve announced it was cutting interest rates by three-quarters of a percent—the largest emergency rate cut in decades. At the time, it was a dramatic policy change. As the year wore on, though, it turned out to be just a small drop in the vast bucket of money that would ultimately be needed to deal with the escalating financial crisis.

Little did Bernanke know that January morning that the thing he feared the most would soon come to pass. As trust unraveled, firms collapsed, markets broke down, and the entire world paid a heavy price with economic activity slowing at an alarming rate.

The financial crisis of 2008 was first and foremost a crisis of integrity. The seeds were sown as great numbers of people sought their own short-term advantage, knowing that they were putting others at risk. In short, it happened like this: Homeowners took out mortgages that they knew were likely to prove unaffordable later on. Banks lent money knowing it was unlikely to be repaid. Wall Street operators bought the junk mortgages and resold them in the guise of sound investments. Accountants, lawyers, and ratings agencies collected hefty fees for misleading assurances. And investors giddily chased outlandish returns, unconcerned by the all too apparent risks. In the climate of greed, frauds great and small multiplied and spread like potent germs in a warm petri dish.

The whole vast and intricate financial universe, with all its sober rules and gray-haired regulators, had been diabolically converted by the nation's brightest minds into a casino where gamblers were risking mountainous piles of other people's money. Before the chips fell, those gamblers claimed a lion's share of false winnings and absconded with fortunes intact, leaving behind a generation's worth of toxic residue for the eventual contemplation of investing clients and the taxpaying public.

Formerly prudent and conservative financial institutions, mighty insurance companies and banks, used loopholes in rules to turn themselves into freewheeling risk takers and in the process ran their firms off the road. Bad strategy and risk taking at the top infected entire institutions and overwhelmed the hard work and diligence of thousands of individual employees. And all the while the true financial state of those institutions was obscured. Banks via reports and balance sheets said over and over that they were solvent, only to reveal later that they actually weren't.

In the end, those in charge compromised the integrity of their institutions and ultimately the integrity of the entire financial system. And they did it while those experts trusted to supervise the system looked the other way.

As soon as investors began questioning the integrity of individual institutions, the financial crisis erupted with a devastating fury. One major bank after another came forward to reveal breathtaking losses, and trust began to unravel. Players who had never questioned each other's integrity did so. Suddenly no one trusted anyone enough to do business with them, and credit markets stopped working. Policy makers and government institutions tried to call on the enormous credibility they had built in the past but instead looked panicked and uncertain. One government initiative after another failed to quell the fear, and investors lost confidence in the people charged with protecting the system itself.

The result of all that integrity and trust unraveling was an economic contraction so profound that it affected every American together with vast populations around the world.

It was a wake-up call. Ignoring or, worse, abusing integrity isn't just unpleasant for a few bad apples and their unlucky victims. It has profound economic consequences. At stake is the entire global economic system, the modern way of life.

. . . . . . . . . . . . . . . . . . . . . . . . . . . . . . . . . . . . . . . . . . . . . . .

## The Cost of the Financial Crisis

### Government Spending in Billions of Dollars as of May 15, 2009

|  | Promised | Provided |
|---|---|---|
| **Total** | 12,080 | 4,036 |
|  |  |  |
| **The Federal Reserve** |  |  |
| Term Auction Credit | 900 | 428 |
| Other Loans: | Unlimited | 132 |
|    Primary credit | Unlimited | 42 |
|    Secondary credit | Unlimited | 0 |
|    Seasonal credit | Unlimited | 0 |
|    Primary dealer credit facility | Unlimited | 0 |
|    Asset-Backed Commercial Paper |  |  |
| Money Market Mutual Fund | Unlimited | 29 |
|    AIG | 46 | 46 |
|    AIG (for SPVs) | 9 | 0 |
|    AIG (for ALICO, AIA) | 26 | 0 |
| Rescue of Bear Stearns* | 27 | 26 |
| AIG-RMBS Purchase Program* | 23 | 16 |
| AIG-CDO Purchase Program* | 30 | 20 |
| Term Securities Lending Facility | 200 | 14 |
| Commercial Paper Funding Facility* | 1800 | 163 |
| TALF | 1000 | 18 |
|  |  |  |
| Money Market Investor Funding Facility | 540 | 0 |
| Currency Swap Lines | Unlimited | 247 |
| Purchase of GSE Debt and MBS | 1250 | 504 |
| Guarantee of Citigroup Assets | 286 | 0 |
| Guarantee of Bank of America Assets | 108 | 0 |
|  |  |  |
| Purchase of Long-Term Treasuries | 300 | 102 |
|  |  |  |
| **Treasury** |  |  |
| TARP | 700 | 570 |
| Fed Supplementary Financing Account | 479 | 479 |
| Backstop of Fannie Mae and Freddie Mac | 400 | 0 |
|  |  |  |
| **Federal Deposit Insurance Corporation** |  |  |
| Guarantee of U.S. Banks' debt:* | 1400 | 349 |
|    Guarantee of Citigroup Assets |  | 10 |
|    Guarantee of Bank of America Assets |  | 2.5 |

| | | |
|---|---|---|
| Transaction Deposit Accounts | 500 | 0 |
| Public-Private Investment Fund Guarantee | 1000 | 0 |
| **Federal Housing Administration** | | |
| Refinancing of Mortgages | 100 | 0 |
| **Congress** | | |
| Economic Stimulus Act of 2008 | 170 | 170 |
| American Recovery and Reinvestment Act of 2009 | 787 | 787 |

*Includes foreign-denominated debt.

Source: Moody's Economy.com

• • • • • • • • • • • • • • • • • • • • • • • • • • • • • • • • • • • • • • • •

# The Economic Value of Integrity

IF MISTAKES ARE learning experiences, the painful lesson from this financial crisis is that integrity really does matter. Not just to our moral well-being but to our economic well-being too.

Integrity is widely misunderstood. Conventionally, integrity is considered an "eat your spinach" topic: a personal issue, entirely up to individuals. If you are upright, good for you; if not, it's no one else's affair. While most people sense that doing the right thing is vaguely beneficial, it's a safe bet they know from personal experience that bending the rules or exploiting loopholes can offer rewards. After all, who hasn't jaywalked or run a red light?

It's easy to point a finger at players in the subprime crisis—mortgage lenders making loans they knew couldn't be paid back, investment bankers peddling junk as if it were prime investments, and ratings agents who signed off on investment products they didn't, or didn't try to, understand—and criticize their lack of integrity. But that's where it usually ends. Little if any thought is given to understanding how integrity affects our economic interests.

This book turns conventional wisdom on its head. The real value of integrity is not personal; it's collective. It's the underpinning for all our commercial relationships. We are heirs to a huge stock of integrity, built up over centuries and visible in every aspect of our economy. It's a shared asset that makes us wealthy.

The dictionary defines *integrity* in terms of adherence to moral principles, rectitude, honor, and honesty. These are certainly admirable qualities. But we need to understand integrity as not simply a virtue but a shared asset that brings financial and economic rewards.

To actually practice integrity, to deal honestly, there has to be someone on the other side of the transaction. That means that to really understand integrity, we have to appreciate it as a relationship of trust.

Once a relationship of trust and integrity exists, remarkable efficiencies result. Partners in trust are spared a multitude of worries—whether they'll get paid, whether they'll get what they think they're paying for. They are freed to act quickly and with confidence, again and again. Pervasive integrity is fundamental to our enormous, fast-moving economy. Integrity isn't something that's nice to have. It's something we have to have.

For without integrity, the economy would not function.

There would be no trading, no credit, no buying or selling. Our modern economy would quickly degenerate into a primitive system, and our wealth would disappear along with it.

Yet we take integrity for granted. We learn from infancy to count on people to tell the truth, keep their promises, and respect others' rights. This trusting attitude is ingrained in American culture, learned from the cradle and accumulated over centuries.

So far, though, the conventional approach to integrity has been to complain about others and punish wrongdoing. That approach might be described as "let's limit the bad stuff people do." But there's another way to think about integrity. What if we invested in integrity? In effect, what if we took a different approach and focused on "increasing the good stuff people do." The ultimate point is that if we invest in our collective integrity, we invest in our collective wealth. We can create wealth together in ways that are not possible alone.

That makes integrity the most valuable asset ever created. And as our greatest asset, it demands careful consideration and a new strategic approach.

| Conventional View of Integrity | Strategic View of Integrity |
| --- | --- |
| *Personal: It's all about you.* | *Collective: It's all about us.* |
| *Private morality.* | *Good economics.* |
| *It'll cost you.* | *It'll benefit you.* |
| *Complain about others.* | *Capture opportunities.* |
| *Punish wrongdoing.* | *Create wealth.* |

## The Pervasiveness of Integrity

DESPITE ALL THE dishonesty, the falsehoods, the cheating, and even the outright fraud we've seen exposed in the world of finance, there's actually a lot of integrity left. Without it, financial activity and the vast majority of commerce would stop completely.

When you examine what's embedded in any transaction, you may never see the world in the same way again. The more you look for integrity, the more you find. Integrity is an unstated assumption in nearly everything we do, from withdrawing cash to investing for our retirement. There's a mountain of integrity out there, and it's what makes the economy go. Yet we hardly ever stop to think about all those people, millions of people, in fact, all around the country, doing the right thing day after day so that everyone can benefit. By focusing on what we do well and on what actually powers economic activity, we can learn to increase it. That means we need to understand what we do right most of the time and how to do more.

If we examine things we take for granted in our daily lives—drinking milk, withdrawing cash, driving a car—we can appreciate how much we depend on the integrity of others. And we can begin to see integrity for what it really is: the invisible infrastructure of the economy. It supports everything we do and is a source of our economic wealth.

One of the biggest hurdles, though, is the notion that doing the right thing will cost you. If you act with integrity, the thinking goes, you probably won't get ahead. That attitude can be particularly prevalent in the corporate world. But some of the biggest corporate success stories have been about companies investing in integrity.

A good example is Toyota and its focus on quality. Rather than focusing on the minimum necessary to sell the product, Toyota has gone above and beyond any carmaker to deliver satisfaction and in the process has become the number one automotive brand in the world. It's a powerful reminder: integrity is an investment and has an economic payoff.

Integrity doesn't just appear by itself nor can it be bought. Integrity is built up over long periods and is passed down through generations. Yet it is fragile and can be destroyed. Those are some of the hard lessons we have learned from the credit crisis. But by understanding the tremendous integrity asset we share, we may then be encouraged to protect and promote it. Acting together, we can make life better for everyone.

## Investing in Integrity

INTEGRITY IS SO crucial to our economic performance that it can explain disparities in national wealth.

Since the United States is one of the wealthiest economies in the world, doesn't that mean we are sitting on something pretty valuable? And shouldn't we understand that? Better yet, if integrity is good for the economy, isn't more integrity better?

Recognizing the economic value of integrity is an essential first step. But the true power of integrity comes not from merely appreciating that it exists, but from knowing how to create more.

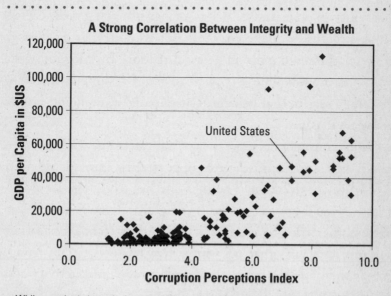

**A Strong Correlation Between Integrity and Wealth**

While a nation's integrity is not readily measured, one measure may be corruption. Using the Corruption Perceptions Index (CPI) calculated annually by Transparency International, it can be found that the higher the CPI index for a nation, the greater the perceived integrity. A chart of 2008 CPI for 180 countries against each one's GDP per capita reveals a strong correlation between corruption and wealth. The higher the level of wealth, the lower the corruption.

Source: 2008 Corruption Perceptions Index from Transparency International, 2008 GDP per Capita from the International Monetary Fund

There's a tendency to throw up our hands when it comes to integrity and appear skeptical that it can, in fact, be encouraged. The truth is that we have the tools right under our nose, and by understanding the DNA of integrity, we can multiply it. It's an empowering realization. We can invest in integrity and in the process create self-reinforcing systems that promote greater integrity and wealth.

In fact, the aftermath of the financial crisis is an ideal opportunity to do just that. When things are going well, there's little incentive to make changes. But when things go wrong, it's a good time to move in a new direction. By knowing what works to promote integrity, we can build a stronger financial system, a system that generates sustainable growth and profits for years to come.

Our conventional approach—"to catch the bad guys"—takes the spotlight off the real opportunity. Instead, we need a new way of thinking. The message has to change from "do right or you'll get caught" to "do right and you'll benefit." A system that tries to eliminate wrongdoing tends to restrict activity. But rules that set people free to do the right thing, rather than holding people back, encourage more activity and create wealth. We should think about it as creating an integrity machine.

Ultimately, we need to acknowledge that the "get ahead at any cost" approach that has been so pervasive in the United States in recent years is not the only way to operate. In fact, it's not even the best way. Doing whatever it takes to get ahead doesn't automatically make the economic pie bigger. Too often, grabbing a larger slice of the pie for oneself comes at the expense of someone else. Investing in integrity is a way of making the pie bigger so that everyone is better off. It's a new way of thinking about the economy. By investing in our shared integrity asset, we can find a new way forward.

## CHAPTER TWO

# It's in the Milk

· · · · · · · · · · · · · · · · · · · · · · · · · · · · ·

One hundred million households do the same thing each morning. The kids dawdle in their rooms, Dad has his head in the newspaper, and Mom is getting breakfast on the table. She reaches into the fridge to get the milk out, tears off a tamper-resistant lid, and pours milk on their cereal. As Mom calls the kids to breakfast, she's not thinking about whether that milk is safe to drink. She knows it is and tells her kids to start eating. Milk is one of the nation's most trusted products. We insist that our children drink milk. If they resist, we pressure them: "Drink your milk and you'll grow up big and strong." That message is reinforced by doctors and nutritionists. They recommend two cups of milk a day for infants and more for older kids.

Yet when we give our children milk, we rarely think of what's involved in bringing that product to our table. Milk is, after all, an animal secretion. And as such, it can harbor dangerous pathogens like bacteria, viruses, and parasites. If milk is not produced carefully, it can cause serious illness and even death.

It wasn't all that long ago that American parents watched as their children sickened and even died from drinking milk. At the beginning of the twentieth century, infant mortality was almost twenty-five times higher than it is today, mostly due to the poor quality of milk, lax production methods, and lack of proper refrigeration. Back then, milk was called "white poison" for the deadly bacteria it could harbor, and illness from milk made up one-quarter of all illnesses caused by contaminated food or water. Today that number is less than 1 percent.

THE CITY MILK BUSINESS.
Mary, the Kitchen-Maid. "Why, John, what's the matter?"
Milkman. "Ah, Mary! if we don't have rain soon, I don't know what we'll do for Milk!"

Yet despite all the innovations and scientific breakthroughs that have increased milk safety over the years, one fact remains: whether you buy your milk from a suburban Wal-Mart, a city convenience store, or directly from a farm, you rely on other people to make certain that the milk is safe to drink. It is amazing how much care goes into a single gallon of milk, and yet we hardly ever stop to think about it. When you drink milk, do you know how much integrity you're depending on?

## It Starts on the Farm

Hours before the sun is up on a crisp fall morning, the lights are on in northern New Jersey's farm country. Inside a large barn, a father and son are getting ready to milk the cows.

The two men don't talk much. They each have a job to do. As one feeds the cows a mixture of hay, corn, and wet brewers' grain (hops, barley, soybeans, and cornmeal), the other gets the milking machines from the storage room and hangs them in position. "C'mon. Get up, girl," the farmer tells a black-and-white cow still lazing on the ground. He prods her gently and then more forcefully: "What's the matter? Get goin', you."

The barn is long and narrow, with cows lined up on each side facing away from the middle. That leaves a center aisle so the men have room to walk up and down as they work. The walls and ceiling are whitewashed, and two pipes run overhead. There are about sixty-five thousand dairy farms all over the country just like this one.

The farmer works quickly, moving from one cow to the next. First he wipes down the teats with soap and water. Then he plugs one hose from the portable milking machine into a stainless-steel pipe that collects the milk and another hose into a second pipe that acts like a vacuum pump. Next he puts the four suction cups onto the cow's teats and presses a button. Instantly the teats are pulled, and milk travels up the hose into the stainless-steel pipe overhead. That pipe is the main artery of the barn. The milk flows through the pipe and is collected in a large storage tank housed in a small room just off the barn.

The machine automatically switches off when the cow has been milked, and the suction cups fall off, signaling to the farmer that he should move to the next cow. After he hooks up the next cow, he comes back and swabs the cow's teats with iodine to prevent infection. "Worst thing for a cow is if you overmilk her," he explains. "That's when you can get bacterial problems."

One and a half hours later, the father and his son have finished milking their last cow—about one hundred in total. Before they come back at 4:00 P.M. to do it all over again, they have to start the cleanup process. The son starts sweeping out the barn, while the father begins collecting the milking machines and putting them in the tank room, where they're connected to a washer. He presses a button so that hot water, detergent, and chlorine rinse out the machines and the stainless-steel pipes overhead, just like a giant dishwasher.

Meanwhile, the warm raw milk that has been collected in the large storage tank was cooled immediately. Cooling is crucial to preventing deadly bacteria from multiplying in the milk. The farmer opens the lid of the tank and checks his output: 5,775 pounds of milk. The rumble of a truck is heard pulling up outside the barn.

## The Pickup

THE PERSON THE farmer depends on most is the milk hauler, who picks up his milk and delivers it to the milk plant. It's his truck pulling up outside the barn at that moment, and the farmer goes to say hello.

A hose appears through a little slot in the wall of the tank room near the floor. The next moment the milk hauler comes in. He's got a stainless-steel container with him called a dipper and he sets it down. He goes straight to the sink to wash his hands.

Next he sets his thermometer in the dipper, which contains a mixture of water and chlorine for washing and disinfecting his equipment.

He takes a clipboard off the wall and removes two stickers, placing them in his documents. He enters the time: 7:45 A.M. He sets down the clipboard and moves to the tank. Opening the tank from a hatch on the top, he peers inside and takes a long sniff. "If there's something wrong with the milk, you can tell by the smell of the tank," he explains. "If there's any odor, then I can refuse to take the milk."

Satisfied that there's nothing unusual about the milk, he moves on to take its temperature.

"Forty degrees. Fine," he says. "If it's over forty, then I have to tell the farmer. There could be something wrong."

Lastly, he pours a small amount of the milk into a pink plastic vial. That sample will be sent to the laboratory at the milk processing plant. If one farmer's milk is tainted, it will spoil the rest of the milk in the tanker. The sample is a way of tracing the source of a contamination.

The driver takes the sample out to the truck and puts it into a small cooler. Over a ten-hour day, he might visit eleven farms and take a sample from each one. The cooler must stay between 33 and 34 degrees Fahrenheit to protect the integrity of the milk samples. He explains that his thermometer has to be recalibrated every month or so to make sure it is accurate.

The driver is almost ready to pump the milk. First, though, he needs to measure how much milk is in the tank.

Inside the farmer's storage tank stands a stainless-steel ruler. The driver turns off the agitator, which keeps the milk from separating, and allows the tank to settle for a moment. He makes a first reading. Then he waits a moment and reads it again. If it's not the same number, he reads it a third time. Then he records the quantity: 5,775 pounds.

He switches on the pump and fills up his truck, which can hold 61,500 pounds of milk. The entire time the milk is in the truck it's kept cool.

Once he's filled his truck, the driver has to seal it. After he has delivered the milk to the plant, the truck is washed thoroughly. To prove it has been cleaned, the truck is given a tag, which must be kept on it until it returns to the plant. The tag says when the truck was washed and by whom. It also includes several seals that the driver must put on all doors to the storage tank to ensure it has not been tampered with. Arriving at the plant without the wash tag or the seals in place means automatic rejection of the milk.

With his tank full, the milk hauler drives back to company headquarters. His day is done when he hands over the keys to a second driver who is just starting his day. This second driver is told from headquarters which dairies to travel to. It could be any number of large dairies in the New York region. It all depends on the demand for raw milk each day.

## At the Milk Plant

ABOUT THIRTY TO forty milk tankers from New Jersey, New York, and Pennsylvania converge at a large plant outside of New York City by midmorning. When a tanker arrives, it clears security at the front gate and proceeds to the check station just steps from the main milk plant.

The tanker is weighed, and a sample of the milk is taken. Before the milk is allowed to be unloaded, the sample is checked in the plant's laboratory. "This is the nerve center of the whole operation," says the head of the lab. Everything that happens in the plant is sampled and tested by him and his team of three lab technicians. The raw milk from each tanker is tested for bacteria, antibiotics, and added water. Its temperature is also taken and must be below 45 degrees Fahrenheit to stop the spread of bacteria. Every lab technician is certified by the Food and Drug Administration. Often the FDA will send blind samples for the lab to check and report back on. At least once a week the FDA has someone visiting the plant to check that all the guidelines are being followed.

All regular milk processed for sale in the United States must comply with the Grade A Pasteurized Milk Ordinance set out by the FDA. The guidelines run into some four hundred pages outlining the quality controls, assurances, and steps in the whole milk production process that must be adhered to in order to sell Grade A pasteurized milk. Developed in the 1920s with a wide range of help from processors, regulators, scientists, machine and equipment suppliers, and researchers, it has become the gold standard for milk safety in the nation.

It takes about fifteen minutes for the tests on the milk sample to be done. If there's a problem with the milk in one of the tankers, the technicians use the individual farm samples collected by the milk hauler to trace the problem. In practice, it's rare for technicians to find a problem. According to the National Milk Producers Federation, the number of tankers found to test positive for animal drug residues when they arrive at the plant is small. In the year ending September 30, 2007, from a total of 3,303,479 milk tanker samples tested, only 1,052 tested positive, or 0.032 percent of the total.

When the driver gets approval from the lab, he's told which part of the pumping station to pull up to. Ten enormous silos hold the raw milk brought into the plant. It takes about half an hour to unload an entire truckload of milk. Once the milk has been pumped out, the truck is washed and cleaned and sent on its way.

The first section of the plant is involved in processing the raw milk. Everything inside this part of the plant is made from stainless steel, and an odor of cleaning chemicals and sterilization predominates. Pipes run down from the ceiling into big enclosed vats and then out the door to the next section of the plant. There's a constant whirr of machines as the milk is pumped down from the silos into the vat where it's heated. For about fifteen seconds the milk is heated rapidly to 161 degrees Fahrenheit, then rapidly cooled. Ultrapasteurized milk is heated to 280 degrees Fahrenheit before rapid cooling. The heat is essential to kill off undesired organisms. After pasteurization, the milk is homogenized. That means the butterfat is broken up into the rest of the milk instead of being allowed to form a thick layer of cream at the top of the milk.

## Milk at a Glance

### Did You Know?

- There are about 11 million dairy cows in the United States producing a total of 21 billion gallons of milk a year, on a total of 65,000 dairy farms in all fifty states.
- The top five producers are:

1. California
2. Wisconsin
3. New York
4. Pennsylvania
5. Idaho

- It takes about two days for milk to go from the cow to the store.
- There are eight different varieties of milk you can buy: whole milk, 2% reduced fat, 1% low fat, fat free, chocolate, evaporated, evaporated fat free, sweetened condensed.

Source: National Milk Producers Federation, National Dairy Council

## The Men Behind Milk

PASTEURIZATION HAS BEEN around since its invention by Louis Pasteur in 1862. The great French scientist had earlier conducted a brilliant experiment in which he exposed boiled broth to air through a filter and showed that spoilage did not occur. This breakthrough proved that airborne germs, not "spontaneous" infection, as previously thought, were the true cause of food-borne illness. With characteristic industry, Pasteur quickly patented the process by which milk would be heated to kill germs and then sealed off to prevent spoilage.

The science of pasteurization has proved to be one of the most important public health advances in history. Yet when it was first introduced, it faced opposition from agricultural industries and a medical establishment that was slow to adapt. In the United States, the widespread adoption of pasteurization waited for half a century after Pasteur's invention. Nathan Straus, a millionaire owner of Macy's department store, was known for progressive business practices and a commitment to public service. Straus had learned that New York City's child mortality increased in the hot summer months. Familiar with Pasteur's work, Straus surmised that spoiled milk played a lethal role. In 1893 he began a twenty-year campaign to make pasteurized and refrigerated milk available to all. He opened depots in New York that distributed pasteurized milk to poor families and conducted a national publicity campaign to encourage the adoption of safe milk production practices. After years of effort, a study ordered by President Theodore Roosevelt in 1908 finally settled the question in favor of modern practices. By 1917, cities across the country had adopted rules requiring pasteurization of milk that are still in force today.

## Bottling Milk

EXAMINE ANY TYPE of packaged food, drink, or medicine today and you'll notice seals that show whether the product has been opened. Tamper-resistant packaging became widespread following the Tylenol scandal that erupted in the fall of 1982 when seven people in the Chicago area were killed after taking Tylenol capsules laced with cyanide. Milk is no exception.

Back at the milk plant, there are two sections for packaging: one for plastic bottles, another for cartons. The bottles enter the building on a conveyor belt, which then transports them to the plant floor to be filled. Each bottle takes only a few seconds to fill and is sealed with a tamper-resistant lid. In an adjoining room, the paper cartons are being filled. Each machine unfolds the carton, which has been stored flat, moves it to the filling station, and seals it up with a circular tamper-resistant lid. Each bottle and paper carton have been coded and dated. By the end of every week, the plant has produced about 1.5 million gallons of milk.

At the lab, scientists sample the final product. While the lab is only required to test the product under ideal conditions, which means after the milk has been refrigerated, the head of the lab instructs his team to stress the product by keeping it at room temperature for twenty-four hours and then testing it.

Meanwhile, rising from the main floor are several conveyor belts with all different sizes and shapes of milk products whirling around to their final destination in the plant: the loading dock. Three large yellow robots pack all the products into pallets. Those pallets are then lifted onto trucks waiting to deliver the milk to retailers. The milk is not allowed to sit on the loading dock. It must remain cool either in the warehouse or in a refrigerated truck.

When the truck arrives at the grocery store, the driver unloads and delivers the milk shipment. It's now up to the storekeeper to keep the milk cold and observe the printed sell-by date. When customers come into the store, they check the date and seal. If it's current and unopened, they don't give the milk another thought.

## Peeling Back the Layers of Integrity and Trust in a Single Gallon of Milk

The milk supply chain reveals how many layers of integrity and trust are embedded in a simple transaction. It's not just the customers who rely on other people when they buy a gallon of milk. Every single person in the chain depends on those who came before in the process, starting with the farmer.

From the milk hauler right on through to the customer, everyone trusts the farmer to look after his cattle and ensure that they are clean and healthy. Dairy cattle need healthy feed to provide the nutritional foundation for the milk. And the milking equipment, machinery, and barn need regular attention.

## Who You Depend On for a Single Gallon of Milk

Farmer
• maintains clean and
  healthy cattle and barn
• cools and stores milk

Feed Supplier
Co-op
Vet
Hoof Trimmer
Nutritionist

Milk Hauler
• test milk
• stores milk

Second Driver
• stores milk
• transports milk
• oversees cleaning of tanker

Milk Plant
• tests milk
• pasteurizes and homogenizes
• packs
• labels

Distributor
• cools and stores milk

Store
• rotates stock
• refrigerates milk

You
• check date
• check lid
• keep cool

To do that, the farmer needs to continually improve his quality and efficiency. He typically does far more than the minimum required to meet the safety standards. Among the experts he hires to improve the quality of milk are the vet, the nutritionist, and the hoof trimmer. The farmer resists overmilking the cattle because he needs to produce milk over the long run. He maintains his barn and ensures that it stays clean. And he follows a daily routine so that he's efficient and his output is reliable.

In turn, the farmer depends on the integrity of everyone else in the chain. He believes the judgment of the experts he consults about the health of the cows. He depends on the reliability of the milking machines and the milk collection and storage systems he has bought. He trusts that the co-op he belongs to has negotiated a fair price for his milk and is maintaining good relationships with the dairies. He trusts the milk hauler to follow the rules so that the farmer's milk is bought by the dairy. At the dairy, the farmer relies on the lab technicians to test the milk accurately and treat the milk safely. He expects that everyone who comes into contact with his milk at the plant, in packaging, and finally in distribution will treat the milk correctly by keeping it refrigerated to prevent any bacteria from growing.

For farmers who operate on a tight budget, it's a matter of survival that all involved do what they're expected to do. Even an interruption of a few days in selling milk can create a serious problem. And yet the farmer doesn't even know in whom he is placing his trust. "We don't really know where our milk goes," he says. "It gets picked up every morning and taken wherever it's needed that day." Dairy farmers rely on the integrity of a whole range of people they never meet so that they can make a living. And they've been doing it for generations.

Farmers in the same neighborhood trust each other to produce good milk. Since milk from seven or eight farms mingles together in the milk tanker, any problem from one farm will contaminate the whole shipment. In that case, the farmer who is found to have the problem must pay the other farmers for the loss of the shipment. But proving where the problem lies depends on the integrity of the milk hauler.

Everyone in the chain trusts that the milk hauler has taken an accurate sample from each farm and that the sample has been preserved properly. They trust that the truck has been maintained after cleaning and is able to keep the raw milk cool during transportation. They depend on the milk hauler recording the relevant information accurately, things like date, time, volume, and temperature. They trust that the milk hauler will drive safely and has an official license to load and unload milk.

The milk hauler has his own extra steps to satisfy himself that the milk is safe and properly accounted for. Sometimes a driver might do more than smell the milk, he'll taste it. Then he checks and rechecks the volume of milk he measures. Once he pumps the milk into his truck, he'll wash out the storage tank for the farmer so it's ready for the afternoon milking.

Everyone in the chain, from the farmer to the consumer, is counting on the lab to test the milk and make sure it is safe. With forty or so tests of raw milk samples a day, hundreds a week, and thousands a month, everyone is relying on the lab and its technicians to administer each test accurately and catch any potential problem in the milk supply. Shopkeepers and consumers expect the plant's labeling to be accurate, and everyone expects the plant to adhere to the FDA rules and regulations.

The lab tests the final products above and beyond what it is required to do to get milk on the table. Plant workers check and recheck the functioning of the machinery to ensure that it works without interruption. After one product goes through processing, that entire part of the plant is washed and rinsed.

The dairy in turn relies on its employees to have the appropriate licensing. The lab technicians, for instance, must all be certified by the FDA. The dairy expects its plant workers to check and recheck that cleaning has been successful and to protect the security of the product. For instance, it trusts its employees not to sabotage the milk by interfering with production or introducing any foreign or harmful substance into the production process. The dairy trusts the delivery trucks to refrigerate the milk and deliver it to the stores that have ordered the final product. It trusts the drivers to treat the milk products carefully and not to damage them in any way. The dairy trusts the store to maintain its milk at cool temperatures and offer only fresh milk to customers. This is important: after all, the dairy's brand name and reputation are on the line. Even in cases where the store is at fault for spoiled milk, the customer may blame the brand and refuse to purchase it again. Finally, the dairy expects customers to react to its product honestly, and not falsely complain or unjustly attack the brand.

It adds up to a huge amount of integrity in a single gallon

of milk. All told, there are about fifteen people who directly control one or another key action to ensure that milk is safe to drink. Then there are people indirectly involved. Think of the company that supplied feed for the cows, the firm that sold the iodine the farmer used to prevent infection, or the antibiotics the vet used to treat the cattle. When you add up all the people indirectly involved in making milk safe, the relationships of trust expand exponentially. There are thousands of people involved in the production of a single gallon of milk, and yet we take it for granted that each one is doing the right thing day after day.

Of course, it's not just milk that depends on relationships of trust. Every aspect of modern life does too. When we get behind the wheel of a car, we trust our lives to the integrity of our fellow drivers. Each driver trusts the other to follow the rules of the road so that we may all arrive safely at our destination. When we fly on an airplane, we depend on thousands of people to make sure the plane arrives safely. Think of the manufacturers of the aircraft, the maintenance crews, air traffic controllers, the pilot, copilot, crew, ground staff, baggage handlers, and so on. And when we sit down to eat at a restaurant, we depend on the integrity of everyone in the kitchen and the cleaning staff, and that all the ingredients used in the meal are fresh and properly cooked.

The number of people we rely on every day to do the right thing is breathtaking. It could easily total in the hundreds of thousands.

# When Something Goes Wrong:
## The 2008 Chinese Milk Scandal

AT THE BEGINNING of 2008, the Chinese dairy industry was booming. Poor farmers scraped together the little they had to buy cows to satisfy the fast-growing demand for milk. Dairies sprang up making a range of products to meet the growing taste of the middle class for Western milk products. Investors bought up the shares of big dairy producers, and foreign dairies rushed to gain a presence in the world's third-largest dairy market. But by year's end, all that had come crashing down.

On July 16, a letter was sent from a Chinese province to the Chinese Ministry of Health, alerting the government to an increase in kidney ailments found in babies drinking Sanlu baby formula. By November, the number of cases had exploded across the nation. Three hundred thousand children were sickened, twelve thousand hospitalized, and six had died from kidney stones and damage related to the chemical melamine, found in milk and infant formula. The World Health Organization said the Chinese milk scandal was the largest food safety event it had ever dealt with.

What's revealing about the Chinese milk scandal is how the economic cost was borne widely and fell in particular on innocent parties. It's not just that Sanlu, the company at the heart of the scandal, collapsed, but almost every other Chinese dairy suffered from weak sales and declining stock prices. While some of those dairies tested positive for melamine in their products, many didn't. The Chinese Dairy Association estimated that industry-wide sales fell 30 to 40 percent in the wake of the scandal and forecast that it would take two years for confidence to be restored. Two million farmers suddenly couldn't support their dairy cows, and many were reported to have slaughtered their livestock as demand for milk dried up. Dozens of countries in Asia and Europe banned Chinese dairy imports. And it was discovered that traces of melamine could be found in other food products in China like eggs, fish, pork, and chicken. Sales suffered in some of those industries too. What's more, since the whole world heard about the scandal and watched images of sickened babies, there was less trust in things made in China in general.

## Why Your Integrity Counts

THE MILK SUPPLY shows that integrity is much more than a personal value. It's a set of relationships. High standards of personal morality won't sell milk, or beef, or any other product, for that matter. There needs to be trust on the other side. If the farmer doesn't operate with integrity, it won't be long before it shows up in the quality of his milk and the dairy refuses to purchase from that farmer. Or if the farmer does everything with the utmost integrity but the dairy doesn't trust him, the dairy won't purchase his milk.

Integrity, then, has two components. The first could be described as trustworthiness—that someone is following the rules, telling the truth, and being careful on the job. The second is trust—believing the seller's trustworthiness. When you have both trustworthiness and trust, you have a relationship of trust and integrity. That relationship—that integrity—is an asset that produces economic value.

In the short term, there's a constant temptation to cut corners to save money or exploit the trust of others. But when one person cuts a corner or exploits the trust of another, it can hurt everyone. If the dairy farmer, for example, overmilks his cows to make more money in the short term, he might end up sickening someone who consumed the milk. If that happened, there could be a wave of fear around the nation about the milk supply, resulting in a cutback in milk consumption that would hurt other dairy farmers, haulers, and producers. And just as in the case of the Chinese milk scandal, it could affect everyone involved in making milk. On the other hand, when all participants in the milk chain do what they say they are going to do—that is, when they act with integrity—they all benefit.

The true economic value of integrity is evident when you view it as a relationship that produces shared benefits. In the case of milk, buyers are confident they are purchasing a safe and effective product, and sellers are able to make a living. But integrity produces benefits in other ways too. Since the milk buyers don't have to test the product or check it in any way, they are freed up to get on with drinking milk and going about their daily lives. The sellers also gain through increased sales and customer loyalty. Integrity works to create wealth by making the economy more efficient.

All those millions of relationships of trust form a vast and intricate web. Those bonds work like a power grid spreading across the nation and charging the economy. Integrity is the invisible infrastructure of the entire economy. It supports everything, holds it together, and allows the economy to work. It's a shared asset that makes us wealthy. Each new relationship of integrity and trust strengthens and grows the economy. Any relationship that breaks down has a ripple effect throughout the system. That means that every individual has the power to make the economy stronger or to weaken it. Your integrity matters. Not just to you but to all of us.

CHAPTER THREE

# Behind the ATM Screen

· · · · · · · · · · · · · · · · · · · · · · · · ·

It seems instantaneous. You insert your card into an ATM, enter a PIN, and request cash. A moment or so later, you're putting that cash in your wallet and walking away, on to the next thing. With ATMs available anytime, anywhere, it's rare to think twice about leaving home without money. In fact, most of us are pretty confident we can withdraw money from our bank account whenever we need to. We trust the bank to deliver our funds, and we depend on that belief.

And yet all it would take is a mere keystroke to alter a bank account. In a second or two, funds could simply vanish from a checking or savings account and records could be lost.

We depend on the integrity of thousands of complete strangers. Most of the time, we don't even know who we're trusting to protect our money, our wealth. We simply trust, in what amounts to an act of blind faith.

That's understandable, though, when integrity is appreciated as a relationship built up over time. Trust doesn't appear by accident but by deliberate efforts made over many years. We are heirs to a huge stock of integrity that has been passed on from one generation to the next. Yet few of us stop to consider the time and effort involved in building up that valuable asset.

For a simple banking transaction like withdrawing money from an ATM, it took close to a century to build the integrity we take for granted today. To understand why, look behind the ATM screen to what actually happens when a cash withdrawal is made. It's a remarkable journey of trust, involving hundreds of strangers you never even see.

## Secure Messages

IT HAPPENS 4 million times a day in the United States. The moment a card is inserted into an ATM, economic activity explodes into life across a vast and intricate web of people bound together in a relationship of integrity and trust.

The ATM immediately deciphers the information hidden in the card's magnetic stripe—your name, card number, and a code for the bank that issued the card—and stores it temporarily. In the same instant, it prompts you for a PIN, or personal identification number. As you key in the numbers, you're actually entering the PIN into a tamperproof chip that stores the secret code. The menu option pops up, and you enter a request for a hundred dollars.

As soon as the machine has the request, it bundles it together with the PIN and account information in the form of a coded message. The message, now ready, is sent through a phone line connecting the ATM with the bank that owns it.

What starts as a message on the phone line continues with more and more parties receiving the message and passing it along. When the bank that owns the ATM receives the initial message, it sends it on to a firm it employs to facilitate ATM transactions. That firm acts like a gatekeeper. It verifies the message and sends it on to the regional ATM network that the bank is a member of.

The network acts like a middleman. It brings together banks so that their customers can use each other's ATMs anywhere in the nation.

If your bank is not a member of the same regional network, the message must be sent on to a national network. At that point, the national network is able to send the message on to your bank for authorization, first through your bank's own regional network, then its gatekeeper, and finally to the bank itself.

Traveling through thousands of miles of phone line, then, the message is stopped, verified, and recorded about eight different times. It's a bit like that game played at children's birthday parties where a secret message is passed on from one person to the next. The difference, though, is that while the child's message almost always fails to reach the last person intact, the ATM message is faithfully preserved as it passes from one participant to the next. It has to be. Otherwise, you wouldn't be able to withdraw your cash.

When your bank receives the bundle of information originally sent from the ATM, it checks the information against your bank account. If there are sufficient funds to meet the request, the transaction is approved and the bank posts a debit to the account.

The message that the transaction has been approved is sent back through the entire eight-member chain in reverse. It is verified and recorded every step of the way until it reaches the ATM. At that point, the machine receives the approval message, the cash door opens, and five crisp twenty-dollar bills roll out.

## Following the Money

YOU TAKE THE cash and walk away. While you think the transaction is done—you have your money, after all—it is actually far from over. There are two more steps still to come; fees need to be paid, and accounts need to be settled, before the transaction is complete.

Ten years ago, few ATMs anywhere in the nation charged user fees. Today, nine out of ten ATMs in the United States charge a fee to users not associated with the ATM owner. If your bank doesn't own the ATM, you might have to pay a few dollars to the local bank for using its ATM. In addition, your bank charges you a fee for using an ATM that isn't part of its network. Both fees are automatically debited from your account.

Then there are all the other fees charged between all parties involved in the transaction. For instance, your bank pays a fee to the ATM's bank, another to its regional network operator, and a third fee to the national network operator. The bank that owns the ATM pays its regional network operator for routing the message and serving as a gatekeeper in the transaction.

Both the fees and the withdrawal itself still have to be settled. That occurs when the funds are cleared through the banking system and all accounts have been adjusted to reflect the transaction.

The five twenties that you put in your wallet are actually lent to you by the ATM's owner until those funds are obtained from your bank. It may feel like your money—you know you have the funds, and you think you're taking it out of your bank account—but you're actually borrowing the money until the owner of the ATM can be repaid.

The process of repayment happens through the Automated Clearing House, a transfer system for electronic payments that connects all financial institutions around the country. Operated by the Federal Reserve, the ACH is like a major airport hub for all electronic payments. Instead of a bank sending a payment directly to another bank, each item gets sent to the ACH, which carefully keeps track and sends it on to its final destination. It's a busy place. On average, $70 billion worth of payments flow through the ACH each day.

Once the Federal Reserve debits or credits the accounts of all those involved in the cash withdrawal, the transaction is settled and done.

## The Growth of ATMs

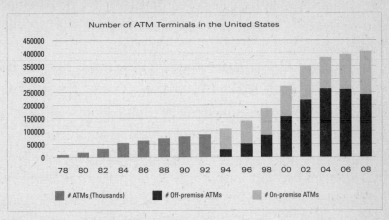

Number of ATM Terminals in the United States

# ATMs (Thousands)   # Off-premise ATMs   # On-premise ATMs

Definitions: On-premise ATMs are ATMs at banks; off-premise ATMs are located off bank premises, such as gas stations, airports, etc. Today, 59 percent of ATMs are located off bank premises.

Source: The Federal Reserve Bank of Kansas City

## Trusting Strangers

WHAT BEGINS AS a journey down the phone line ultimately involves thousands of people who don't know you or even each other, working together to ensure that your transaction is successful. It only takes one person to do the wrong thing for the transaction to fail. And yet that rarely happens. Every minute, every day, all those strangers are doing exactly what they said they would do so that we can withdraw money from our bank accounts at home or away from home.

At each step in the authorization process, a party receives the message to withdraw one hundred dollars along with all the secret identification information, trusts the information, and faithfully sends it along to the next party. Once the authorization decision is made, every party receives the message to give you cash, trusts the message, and faithfully sends it on back down the chain.

The entire time, those parties are passing along valuable information such as PINs and bank account details. At no point does anyone provide false information, steal secure information, or treat the information carelessly. Instead, it is protected and passed along. It's a bit like handing over cash to a friend when that cash needs to be passed on from one person to another until it gets back to the owner. The thing is, with an ATM transaction, some of the parties you trust to handle your money are complete strangers you may only encounter once and never again. It would seem like a perfect opportunity to take a bit of your money or somehow benefit at your expense. Yet on a consistent basis, that doesn't happen.

When it comes to fees, each party provides a service first and gets paid later. The parties are able to provide the service immediately and without hesitation because they are acting on the firm belief that they will be paid. Even at the ATM, you agree to pay a fee to the owner of the machine, but that fee won't be paid until long after the transaction is complete and you leave with your cash. When you hit "I agree" to the transaction fee, you are actually making a promise to pay that the ATM owner trusts.

Not only do the parties involved in the transaction expect to get paid, when they do get paid they expect to get the fee that was negotiated ahead of time. Not a penny less.

During settlement of the transaction, information is tallied precisely and faithfully reported to the next member of the settlement chain. Any inaccuracies would create significant complications for the parties seeking to be paid. At a minimum, it could delay payment. A report of a different amount might even be hard to prove, and an inaccuracy could become a reality. The only way the Automated Clearing House works is if everyone involved honestly reports the payment amounts. To ensure that that occurs, all institutions promise to abide by the rules of the ACH, and in return all expect that the Federal Reserve will accurately credit or debit their accounts by the correct amount.

In addition to all the other relationships of integrity and trust needed to make this single transaction work, there's the relationship between your bank and the ATM's bank.

The ATM's bank trusts that your bank will repay the hundred dollars it just handed out without even knowing the identity of your bank first. Think about that for a moment. There are probably hundreds of transactions occurring daily at any one ATM. The owner of the ATM can't know every bank in advance, but simply trusts it will be repaid regardless of which bank is involved in the transaction. In turn, your bank trusts that the ATM is being properly maintained and that you are in fact who you say you are.

When you use an ATM, you have a high degree of trust in the owners of that machine. You trust that your PIN will not be stolen or accidentally given out to anyone else. Moreover, you display enormous trust in your own bank. You expect that the bank will allow you to withdraw funds from your account at any time and that the bank will maintain that account accurately and carefully to reflect all transactions.

In total there are twelve key relationships of integrity and trust embedded in a simple ATM withdrawal.

It's critical to appreciate that every one of those relationships was built over time. They didn't suddenly appear by accident. Those relationships were intentionally created by the cooperation of many individuals, often involving lengthy efforts and at times as a result of widespread problems or negative experiences.

Every one of those twelve relationships is critical for the ATM transaction to succeed, and each can be traced back to reveal exactly how it was built up. Consider just one of those relationships—trust between you and your bank. Why do we trust banks with our money?

## The Rise of the Bank Account

OPENING UP A bank account takes a pretty big leap of faith. You hand over your money to a complete stranger and ask that stranger to look after it. Yet we do it all the time. In fact, it's become a completely unremarkable part of modern life. Thinking about what's at stake is staggering. Today the public keeps billions of dollars in bank accounts. All that money in someone else's hands; all that trust.

While about nine out of ten Americans have a bank account today, it wasn't always that way. Much of the nation's

## How Many Relationships of Trust Are in an ATM Withdrawal?

**You**

**ATM**

You and ATM

You and your bank

ATM provider and ATM's bank

Gatekeeper and ATM's bank

Gatekeeper and network

Network and national network

ATM bank and Automated Clearing House

ATM's bank and your bank

Gatekeeper and your bank

Gatekeeper and your bank's network

Your bank's network and national network

Your bank and Automated Clearing House

**Total: Twelve Relationships of Trust**

history was characterized by a deep distrust of banks. Ordinary Americans often preferred to keep their savings in some tangible form—land, goods, or gold—rather than hand it over to a bank. At the turn of the twentieth century, only about one in ten Americans had a bank account.

So what happened to change that?

The transformation didn't happen overnight. Americans

didn't wake up one morning and suddenly decide that they would trust banks with their hard-earned money. Nor did banks, for their part, suddenly wake up and decide it would be good business to let everyone open a bank account. It was a gradual, decades-long process by which a relationship of integrity and trust was built between banks and the American public. And at times that relationship was tested. During the Great Depression, it was badly damaged and had to be rebuilt. But those difficult times led to some of the biggest steps ever made in promoting integrity. By looking back, it becomes apparent which events or policies have promoted integrity and which have undermined it. What's more, a look at the past shows that the evolution of integrity is not always smooth or even, yet over time integrity advances.

## DEEP DISTRUST

For most of the nation's history, almost a century and a half, ordinary Americans were deeply suspicious of banks. From the birth of the nation right up to World War I, the vast majority of Americans had few direct dealings with banks, and what they heard or knew of banks wasn't good.

Up until World War I, most Americans had little in savings, and what they had they weren't about to hand over to a bank. Only professionals, merchants, manufacturers, and farmers tended to have bank accounts. Everyone else did without.

It wasn't as if banks were a new phenomenon. They had been around since the birth of the nation. The first bank opened its doors in Philadelphia in July 1780. Called the Pennsylvania Bank, it was largely needed to help finance the fight against the British and was championed by Alexander Hamilton. Some eleven years later, the first national bank was created, the Bank of the United States, and with it the beginning of deposit banking in the new nation.

From the beginning, though, the nation's leaders were deeply mistrustful of banks. Thomas Jefferson was famously quoted as saying, "The object of the latter [banks] is to enrich swindlers at the expense of the honest and industrious part of the nation." And John Adams said, "Banks have done more injury to the religion, morality, tranquility, prosperity, and even the wealth of a nation than they can have done or ever will do good."

Fifty years after the first bank opened its doors, Andrew Jackson, the president at the time, waged an epic battle to destroy the only national bank in the country, the Second Bank of the United States. Jackson was victorious, and that episode was seen as a major victory of the people over the banks.

The remainder of this long period of distrust was characterized by one bank panic after the other. Much of what the public heard from its leaders was backed up by the experience of seeing lines forming outside banks in what amounted to frequent banking crises.

There were five banking crises between 1870 and 1914 alone: in 1873, 1884, 1890, 1893, and 1907. One bank failure often resulted in widespread panic and quickly spread to other banks, as expectations of future failures and a crisis of confidence took hold.

As for commercial banks, their relationships through much of the history of the nation were with business leaders and professionals. They didn't try to win over the general public. In fact, they didn't trust the public to be a reliable source of deposits.

## A Relationship Emerges

World War I began to change the public's relationship with banks. Between 1914 and 1921, many Americans opened up their first bank account.

Demand for weapons, food, manufactured goods, and transportation had been a boon for American production, and money came pouring into the nation. With increased prosperity, ordinary people had more funds than before, and banks opened up in towns where they had never previously existed. Thousands of people who had never had any prior experience with banks were having their first taste.

At the same time, this was the era when the Federal Reserve System was created to encourage stability in the banking sector and the broader economy, adding to the public's confidence.

## Confidence Shattered

Six years later, though, the public's newfound relationship with banks began to sour. Beginning in the fall of 1920, an economic crisis swept the nation. Although it was a brief economic contraction, lasting less than a year, it was severe.

Wholesale prices, industrial production, and the manufacturing sector suddenly collapsed, putting stress on many small banks ill-equipped to survive the severe downturn. This marked the beginning of a thirteen-year period in which integrity was undermined and trust shattered, as across the nation banks small and large failed, wiping out much of the public's savings.

It started in the Roaring Twenties. While much of the country prospered, this period was remarkable for the extraordinary number of small banks that failed, which hurt ordinary Americans the most. Suddenly big banks were thriving while small banks were not. As firms grew, they were able to utilize the stock and bond markets to raise capital. Big banks moved into the business of underwriting stocks and bonds, but small banks could not. In addition, the importance of agriculture to the economy declined, hurting many small banks.

While the number of commercial banks had been growing from about 1914 onward, that trend changed suddenly around 1921. In 1914 there were twenty-seven thousand commercial banks. That number grew to thirty thousand in 1921 before falling below twenty-five thousand by 1929. While there were only five hundred reported bank failures from 1915 to 1920, from 1921 to 1929 the number of failures jumped to six thousand.

According to financial and economic historians, a large fraction of the banks that collapsed had capital of twenty-five thousand dollars or less and were located in towns of twenty-five hundred people or fewer, mostly in western grain states.

This period of small-bank failures helped to undermine the confidence of ordinary Americans in the banking system and laid the groundwork for the subsequent runs and big-bank failures that were just around the corner. People who held deposits in banks that failed often never saw that money again. There were no guarantees or insurance to protect their savings.

In October 1930, bank failures in Missouri, Indiana, Illinois, Arkansas, and North Carolina led to a contagion of fear of more bank failures around the nation. The first of the big-bank failures occurred on December 11, 1930, when the Bank of the United States, with over $200 million of deposits, collapsed. Then there was a second banking crisis in 1931 followed by another in 1933.

During this period, one-third of banks simply vanished, along with people's savings. Ordinary people who had never deposited money in banks before watched as they and their neighbors lost everything. The experience was searing, and the brief relationship of integrity and trust the public had developed with the banks since the war was broken. It would take decades to rebuild.

## Trust Rebuilt

Rebuilding the public's trust in banks meant monumental changes to the banking industry, with some of those changes continuing to produce lasting benefits even today.

In 1933, cleaning up the banking sector began in earnest with a series of emergency measures to stabilize the banking system.

President Roosevelt instituted a nationwide banking holiday from Monday, March 6, to Monday, March 13. During that time, all commercial banks and the Federal Reserve Banks were closed. To reopen, banks had to apply for a license and submit to checks by authorities before they were pronounced clean.

At the beginning of 1933 there were 17,800 banks. After the bank holiday there were only 12,000 licensed banks. The rapid cleanup of the banks and the official licensing requirement gave the public confidence that banks with a license were safe to do business with—in other words, that they would repay customer deposits.

In addition, the Reconstruction Finance Corporation was established to inject capital directly into licensed banks that still needed capital. The RFC invested a total of $1 billion in bank capital, which amounted to one-third of the total capital of all banks in the United States in 1933. It also made loans amounting to $2 billion to distribute to depositors who had lost money in bank failures.

Then there were more lasting reforms. The most important was the establishment of the Federal Deposit Insurance Corporation in 1933 as part of the Glass-Steagall Act. Economic historians believe that this was the single most successful policy in the history of the nation for achieving what had never been achieved before: the prevention of industry-wide bank panics.

The FDIC insured deposits of banks, giving small depositors in particular the confidence that even if a bank was having financial difficulties, their deposits were not at risk. It became effective on July 1, 1934, with an initial level set at a maximum of twenty-five hundred dollars for each depositor. All banks that were members of the Federal Reserve System were required to have their deposits insured by the FDIC, while those that weren't could also apply. Within six months, 97 percent of all commercial bank deposits were covered by insurance. Over time, the level of deposits insured by the FDIC has been raised. Starting on July 1, 1934, it was raised to five thousand dollars. In September 1950, it was raised again to ten thousand dollars. By 2009 the limit stood at two hundred thousand dollars.

In addition to the FDIC, the Glass-Steagall Act required the separation of banks into commercial and investment banks. At that time, it was widely recognized that the investment banking activities taken on by commercial banks in the boom had destabilized the banking industry and made commercial banks extremely risky. The separation between commercial and investment banks remained in place until 1999, when it was repealed.

The last far-reaching change was to the Federal Reserve System itself. The central bank was blamed for exacerbating the crisis. Critics believed that its structure meant that decision making was diffused through the twelve regional banks and had become ineffectual. The Banking Act of 1933 brought the power of the Federal Reserve to Washington and away from the twelve regional banks. The Federal Reserve was also granted greater power over commercial banks, being able to change reserve requirements as it saw fit.

## A STRONG BOND

Thirty years later, banks built on that renewed trust to forge an even closer relationship with American households. A little-known public figure in the Kennedy administration, James Saxton, almost single-handedly transformed the banking industry in the 1960s. As comptroller of the currency, he introduced sweeping changes that allowed banks to compete more aggressively against each other.

A backdrop of strong economic growth, benefiting households, and a wave of competition from banks led to the beginning of a boom in consumer lending. Lending to consumers strengthened the relationship banks had with households and transformed the checking account into an unremarkable necessity of modern life.

The relationship of trust between you and your bank, built over generations, is essential for an ATM withdrawal to take place. Yet it's only one out of a dozen relationships that are necessary for that single transaction to succeed. ATMs require trust in many people and systems. For instance, there's trust between banks, trust between the Automated Clearing House and banks, trust between ATM networks, and our own trust in the ATM operator.

By examining one aspect—the trust between the public and banks—we can see that time has been a key factor in the development of a relationship, but on occasion particular policies have helped to promote growth in that relationship too.

The big changes, in particular those instituted after the Great Depression, increased the integrity of the banks markedly and as a result the public's trust. Primarily because of the creation of the FDIC and deposit insurance, Americans no longer fear that they can lose money kept on deposit at banks.

That has been a big help in maintaining public confidence in banks, especially during the financial crisis of 2008. While the stock price of many commercial banks plummeted due to enormous losses from mortgage lending and other loans tied to property, the deposit base was relatively stable, as Americans trusted they would have access to their funds even in times of severe financial distress.

Almost one hundred years after ordinary Americans first began a fledging relationship with banks, they trust they will be able to access their money even when the banks are on the brink of failure. Giving Americans that confidence has been essential for promoting stability in the banking system.

Today, when you insert your card into an ATM, you're not thinking about all that trust, built up over decades through the hard work of individuals and government. Integrity then doesn't appear by accident. It takes the efforts of many people over a long time to build. That's an empowering realization. If individuals and governments in the past have built integrity, we can too.

## CHAPTER FOUR

# Good as Gold

· · · · · · · · · · · · · · · · · · · · · · · · · · · ·

At 8:30 A.M. on a workday in lower Manhattan, the financial hub of the world, people spill out of the subway on their way to Wall Street. Some are clutching coffee, others a newspaper, as they pass by an imposing stone edifice that looms over the narrow streets. As people dash to the office, thoughts turn to the day ahead. Few probably realize that beneath their feet lies the greatest treasure trove in the world.

Deep down in the bedrock of the island of Manhattan, about eighty feet below street level, is an impenetrable steel-encased vault. Spanning nearly two-thirds of an acre, roughly half the size of a football field, it belongs to the Federal Reserve Bank of New York.

The vault contains gold. Piles of it. One-quarter of all the gold in the entire world is locked away for safekeeping within its walls. As the price of the precious metal has skyrocketed in recent years, so too has the value of all that gold. In 2008, it was worth close to $200 billion.

Very little of the gold belongs to the United States. In fact, from time to time some of it has even belonged to the nation's warring enemies. Yet for nigh onto a century the Federal Reserve Bank of New York has served as guardian of the world's gold, protecting the metallic wealth of other nations despite wars, bitter international disputes, and terrorist attacks. So why does the bank protect all that gold? It's an intriguing question, considering that the Federal Reserve Bank of New York doesn't charge a dime for safeguarding the world's bullion.

Some countries made gold deposits at the vault from as early as 1924, but it wasn't until the threat of World War II that many first shipped over their reserves. At the time, the United States was seen as a safer place than Europe—physically separate and politically stable—and New York was growing in importance as a financial center. By keeping that gold safe over decades, the bank has gained the trust of the rest of the world. That trust has been incredibly valuable—something that generations of Americans have benefited from and continue to benefit from today.

## Getting into the Bank

GAINING THAT TRUST requires an extraordinary vault. There's only one way in or out of the vault, and that's through the bank's headquarters at Liberty Street and Maiden Lane.

The building is more than a little forbidding, made from large limestone and sandstone slabs. Huge windows covered with wrought-iron bars warn the public to keep out. Built in 1922, the bank was designed after the palaces of Florence that date from the Italian Renaissance and the age of the Medici bankers. While the building is grand, it looks much more like a fortress than a palace.

Tough-looking security guards armed with guns patrol the front steps, suspiciously eyeing anyone who gets a little too close. Each security guard is a qualified marksman. The bank has its own firing range within the building where guards are expected to maintain their shooting skills.

Visitors must explain their business to a guard before being allowed to take a step in the direction of the front door. Given the nod, they proceed up the broad front steps of the bank past huge wrought-iron lanterns created by master artisans from an earlier era.

Guarding the large arch of the bank's main entrance are heavy front doors of teak recessed into the side of each wall. At the press of a button, in a mere seven seconds, these massive doors can be shut. In thirty seconds, the bank itself can be locked down completely, a situation that last occurred during the September 11 terrorist attacks.

Visitors place all belongings on a scanner and walk through a metal detector. Once cleared, they're sent to the front desk, manned by another security agent. There's no warm welcome. No smiles here.

Nobody gets into the bank without being on a list. Members of the public touring the gold vault must make an appointment in advance and provide ID over the Internet. All other visitors are invited. The guard asks for a driver's license. Once it's handed over, he makes a copy and uses it to produce a picture ID security pass.

The stone lobby is vast and austere. A bronze statue of the ancient Greek tragedian Sophocles, on loan from the Metropolitan Museum of Art, maintains a silent watch. A sign warns: "All cameras must be checked. If pictures are taken, the film will be confiscated."

## Deep Down into the Vault

VISITORS TO THE gold vault are escorted by an employee of the bank.

Traveling five floors down by elevator, the doors open on a gray vestibule with a single, electronically locked door. Using a security card, the guide opens the door into a corridor lined with pictures and explanations of the special features of the vault and the building. That corridor leads directly to the vault's entrance.

No notebooks, pens, or paper of any description is allowed into the vault. Visitors have to leave all their personal belongings, including handbags, on a table before entering.

There's only one way in, through a narrow passageway. Made from 280,000 pounds of steel, it's the passageway that really protects the vault. A large steel hand wheel just outside the passageway on the left controls the accessibility of the vault. To close the vault, a guard spins the wheel four times around, rotating a ninety-ton steel cylinder to block the passageway. Another guard spins a second steel wheel on the right-hand side of the passageway sixty-four times around to lower the ninety-ton cylinder three-eighths of an inch into the ground. That creates an airtight and watertight seal for the vault. A third guard presses special levers that insert four rods into individual holes within the cylinder, triggering a time clock system. The vault is shut tight until the time on the clock has elapsed.

Walking through the steel passageway, visitors find themselves right inside the vault. There are no windows and no doors. Everything is painted a sober gray. Incredibly, the vault itself, built in 1924, is as impenetrable today as it was back then. A masterpiece of engineering, foresight, and brute force, it has stood the test of time. No one has ever tried to rob the vault.

The vault is carved into the bedrock of Manhattan and lined with steel-reinforced concrete. Of utmost importance to the engineers at the time was that the vault be able to support the weight of the structure itself in addition to the gold, about seven thousand tons in total. Manhattan's bedrock is one of the few secure places that can do that.

Just inside the passageway, visitors are confined by walls of bars much like a prison cell. Only a handful of people may go any farther, and those are the trusted Fed staffers who are responsible for the vault. Everyone else must peer in from a safe distance. Otherwise, a range of hidden cameras, motion detectors, and silent alarms would trigger an immediate response from the bank's security team.

Peeking through the bars, visitors can hear a faint rumble from the subway overhead, the only real reminder of the outside world.

## Stacks of Gold

STEEL CAGES LINE the vault. On the outside of each compartment are a padlock, two combination locks, and an auditor's seal. The seal is an assurance that everything inside is as it should be.

Inside, each cage is stacked high with gold bricks. Each brick is about 7 inches long, 3½ inches wide, and around 1¾ inches thick. They're just a bit smaller than the common bricks used in the construction of homes but far heavier. When gold is used as a store of wealth, it's kept in the form of bars or bricks. Bricks are easier to count, store, and transport. The gold bricks are stacked like regular construction bricks on wooden pallets. The impression is more of construction material than precious metal.

In total, there are 540,000 gold bricks inside the vault. It's worth imagining for a moment what all that gold looks like. If it were possible to stack up the gold into a single pile, it would extend for about twelve miles. Or take the tallest building in New York City. All that gold would make forty stacks as high as the Empire State Building.

At 2008 prices, each brick would be worth between $275,000 and $375,000. So holding three bars would be the same as holding $1 million.

Each gold brick tells a story. Its shape reveals whether it was cast in the United States or internationally and during what time period. Rectangular bricks were cast in the United States prior to 1986, while trapezoidal bars are newer or cast abroad.

## What Is Gold Used For?

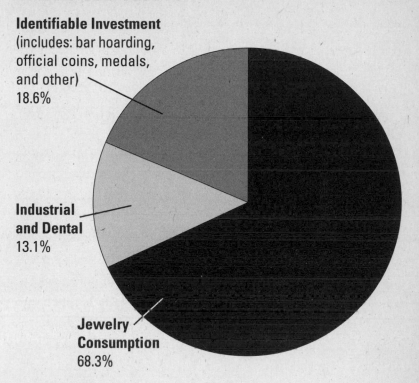

**Identifiable Investment**
(includes: bar hoarding,
official coins, medals,
and other)
18.6%

**Industrial
and Dental**
13.1%

**Jewelry
Consumption**
68.3%

The world's demand for gold in 2007 excluding central banks
Source: GFMS Ltd and World Gold Council

Any individual brick will have a series of markings that explain the year and the location where it was cast as well as its purity level. No gold bar is 100 percent pure, as gold at that level would be far too soft to retain its shape. Instead, the purity of any bar is between 99.5 percent and 99.9 percent, and it contains small quantities of other metals like silver, copper, iron, or nickel.

Gold has a pretty high density, so any bar feels a lot heavier than it actually is. Each gold bar weighs on average 28 pounds, about the weight of a two-year-old child. But the high density makes the bar feel more like 50 pounds, the weight of a healthy six-year-old. Falling bricks are a danger. The concrete floor is scarred and dented where bricks have dropped.

When the gold first arrives at the vault, each bar is weighed and measured for purity. This step is crucial since it determines the value and acceptability of the gold in international transactions. Once the gold is inspected, weighed, measured, and its serial number recorded, it won't be checked again. That's it. So it has to be done thoroughly and carefully and recorded accurately. It requires a pretty unusual scale. Designed in the 1920s, the scale has been a main feature of the vault since it first opened. It has big teardrop buckets that can hold stacks of gold. Several years ago, an employee accidentally bumped into the scale, throwing off its calibration. It took several months before the bank was able to find someone who could fix it. In the meantime, the bank used its smaller electronic scale, which is very precise. It weighs each bar to the nearest one-thousandth of an ounce.

Each of the 122 cages that house the bullion looks the same. There's no name or lettering on the outside, only a number. The bank keeps the identity of gold depositors a secret. Only a handful of the twenty-seven hundred people who work for the Federal Reserve Bank of New York actually know who keeps their gold in the vault. Even those who actually handle the gold and shift it around the vault aren't allowed to know who owns it. Publicly, the Federal Reserve has revealed that the gold belongs to forty-eight foreign nations along with twelve international institutions, like the International Monetary Fund and the World Bank.

The United States, which owns about one-quarter of the world's gold reserves, keeps only a very small fraction of that with the New York branch of the Federal Reserve. Most of its bullion is kept at Fort Knox, Kentucky, and West Point, New York, with smaller amounts at federal government buildings in Denver, Philadelphia, and San Francisco.

. . . . . . . . . . . . . . . . . . . . . . . . . . . . . . . . . . . . . . . . . . . . .

## The World's Official Gold Holdings (March 2009)

### The 25 Biggest Gold Reserves

| Country or Institution | Tonnes | % of total |
| --- | --- | --- |
| United States | 8,133.50 | 27 |
| Germany | 3,412.60 | 11 |
| International Monetary Fund | 3,217.30 | 11 |
| France | 2,487.10 | 8 |
| Italy | 2,451.80 | 8 |
| Switzerland | 1,040.10 | 4 |
| Japan | 765.20 | 3 |
| Netherlands | 612.50 | 2 |
| China | 600.00 | 2 |
| European Central Bank | 536.90 | 2 |
| Russia | 523.70 | 2 |
| Taiwan | 423.60 | 1 |
| Portugal | 382.50 | 1 |
| Venezuela | 363.90 | 1 |

| | | |
|---|---|---|
| India | 357.70 | 1 |
| United Kingdom | 310.30 | 1 |
| Lebanon | 286.80 | 1 |
| Spain | 281.60 | 1 |
| Austria | 280.00 | 1 |
| Belgium | 227.50 | 1 |
| Algeria | 173.60 | 1 |
| Philippines | 153.90 | 1 |
| Libya | 143.80 | 0 |
| Saudi Arabia | 143.00 | 0 |
| Sweden | 135.90 | 0 |
| **World** | **29,691.70** | **92** |

Source: World Gold Council

. . . . . . . . . . . . . . . . . . . . . . . . . . . . . . . . . . . . . . . . . . . . . .

## When Gold Changes Hands

IT IS ONE thing to look after your own treasure but quite another when it's somebody else's. There's more pressure, more responsibility.

Not only does the Federal Reserve store gold, but it also carries out international gold transactions. These trades are a world apart from the high-speed computer-based transactions that characterize global markets these days. When a depositor wants to buy or sell gold from another nation, it notifies the New York Fed about the details of the transaction, such as amount and timing. The Fed officials who oversee the gold vault then assemble and direct a team of "gold stackers" to shift the gold from one compartment to another.

The amount is carefully counted out, and the bricks are stacked on a trolley. The gold is then wheeled over to another nation's locker and carefully stacked inside. To protect their feet, stackers wear magnesium shoe covers. These are lightweight, so they can still maneuver around, but extremely strong, to protect their feet from being severely crushed by falling gold.

Sometimes large trolleys carrying piles of gold bricks are left sitting in a corridor as if forgotten. Usually that happens when a transaction is taking place, because moving the bricks from one place to another can be slow and laborious.

The entire time the transaction is taking place, the stackers know only to move the gold from one numbered compartment to another. The identity of the nations involved in the transaction isn't discussed.

"Everything that happens in the vault is based on trust," says the guide. It's remarkable that in the eighty years since the gold vault was first opened, only one depositor has ever asked to check its gold.

## Leaving the Vault

WHEN A NATION wants to make a gold withdrawal, it notifies the bank. A team of three trusted staffers oversees the procedure. These key people are known as the "control group," and they are present when any activity takes place in the vault. One member is chosen from each of three sections of the bank: auditing, vault services, and custody.

Those jobs aren't easy to come by. Anyone wanting to work in the gold vault is required to have been an employee at the New York Fed for a minimum of fifteen years. And every employee undergoes a background investigation before being hired.

During a transaction, the control group is effectively joined at the hip. Nothing can take place without all three being present. A joke at the bank is "How many people does it take to change a lightbulb in the gold vault?" The answer: "Four: one technician and three Fed staffers to watch." Any time the gold is moved or someone enters the vault, the three-member control group is present. Even when the vault is cleaned, about once a month, the group is there to supervise.

Each compartment must be unlocked by all three at the same time. There are three locks on every compartment door: two combination locks and one padlock. The bank calls its system "triple control."

Once the compartment is unlocked, the door is opened. Opening the compartment door signals an alarm in the central guardroom, where security guards monitor the entire operation. To make a withdrawal, the staff must verify the records that have come with the gold and ensure that there are no discrepancies. If all records match, guards take the gold on trolleys to a freight elevator. A bank employee operates the elevator from a control room and talks with the guards via intercom the whole time. If everything is in order, he allows the guards to proceed out of the elevator.

The gold goes off the freight elevator at the main loading

dock of the bank and into an armored car. Once the armored car drives away, the gold is no longer the responsibility of the bank.

Over the years, very little of the gold stored in the vault has actually left the bank. Much of it has remained at the Federal Reserve since the vault opened.

## Winning the World's Trust

THE GOLD VAULT indicates the importance the Fed places on its own integrity. Intricate locking and security systems, rules, procedures, and triple checks are just some of the great lengths the bank goes to in order to protect all that wealth. It also shows how integrity can be built from many small details.

But what's really behind the integrity of the Fed? It's the people who work there. Hundreds of individuals help oversee the operation of the vault, ensuring the safety of the world's gold. Security guards, accountants, and bankers all work together using procedures like triple control and careful monitoring to maintain the trust of depositors.

Beyond the integrity of the people directly involved, though, lies the trust the rest of the world places in the system of law, order, and government of the United States. Depositors believe that if someone at the Fed does something wrong, it can be addressed under the law. They expect that the entire legal system, from law enforcement officers to judges, courts, and jails, will operate if necessary to address any problems. And the integrity of the legal system is ultimately backed by the government of the United States, which controls the law and the people who administer those laws.

Crucially, depositors don't fear that their gold will be seized by the U.S. government. They count on the government to respect their rights, and they don't worry about a breakdown in the legal or political system of the nation.

The trust of foreign nations in the Federal Reserve Bank of New York's gold vault is ultimately derived from the trust those same nations place in the U.S. government and its people.

## From Gold to the Wealth of Nations

WHEN THE FEDERAL Reserve Bank of New York first started looking after gold back in the 1920s, bullion was at the center of the international financial system. At the time, gold was crucial to the way nations traded because the value of currencies was determined by a nation's gold reserves. Gold transactions occurred frequently, and the security and operation of the gold vault were an important part of the health of the international system.

Being guardian of the world's gold helped build up the credibility of the Federal Reserve Bank of New York and enhanced the status of the entire Federal Reserve System.

Decades later, the gold vault is in some ways a relic of the past. After 1974, the world moved away from the gold standard, or gold exchange, to a system where currencies fluctuate on the open market. Buyers and sellers of a country's currency determine its value instead of gold.

Yet the central bank's success in protecting the gold of nations paved the way for its influence in global currency markets. Today gold makes up only a minuscule fraction of the many transactions the Federal Reserve Bank of New York conducts for the rest of the world.

The Fed overseas billions of dollars in dollar-denominated transactions daily for foreign nations. On any given day, the bank may invest around $55 billion on behalf of other nations and ensure the safekeeping of trillions of dollars. In essence, the Federal Reserve Bank of New York operates a bit like a bank to the whole world, buying, selling, and safeguarding assets for other governments as well as for our own government in the United States. It was a natural transition. The guardian of the world's gold became the guardian of the modern world.

## The Economic Value of the Federal Reserve

THE CREDIBILITY THE bank earned as guardian of the world's gold has played a role in building credibility in global financial markets. Today the Fed holds a unique position among central banks. No other central bank in the world is as admired or respected as the Federal Reserve. That exalted position gives the Fed enormous power and influence in the financial system as well as valuable knowledge of the international marketplace.

All that integrity built up at the Federal Reserve over decades delivers impressive economic benefits for Americans. Through its role in facilitating the global financial transactions of foreign governments, the Federal Reserve helps to promote world trade and a stable international financial system. That benefits American businesses and consumers, promoting economic growth. Another benefit has been to the city of New York itself. Through its significant role in world markets, the Fed has helped build the city into a global financial hub, attracting investment and savings from all over the globe.

Then there are the tremendous economic benefits from the central bank's critical role in conducting monetary policy. When the board of governors of the Federal Reserve decides to lower or raise official interest rates, it's the Federal Reserve Bank of New York that actually makes it happen by buying and selling U.S. government securities. That ability to manage the economy through financial markets has been crucial to smoothing out business cycles and promoting long-term economic prosperity in the United States. The collective knowledge and skill of the New York Fed ensures that monetary policy is carried out successfully.

At those times when the Federal Reserve conducts monetary policy, it can use its influence to nudge the market without actually having to raise or lower interest rates. Former Fed chairman Alan Greenspan was a master at getting the market to do his work for him. If he wanted to ease credit conditions, a few well-chosen words could be as effective as lowering official short-term interest rates. Other nations' central bankers simply don't have the same sway. As a result of all that accumulated trust, the Fed has more flexibility in how it conducts monetary policy and can take steps not available to other nations.

The strong degree of trust other nations have in the Federal

Reserve allows the bank to lead and coordinate international policy efforts in times of distress in the international financial system. For much of 2008, for instance, the Federal Reserve coordinated the efforts of major central banks to pump money into the global system in order to prevent markets from seizing up. If the U.S. central bank had not had the trust and respect of others, it could never have achieved that coordinated rescue effort.

In the midst of a financial and economic crisis, having the trust of the rest of the world is extremely valuable in other ways too. In effect, other nations and investors give the Federal Reserve the benefit of the doubt in dealing with policy problems. This provides crucial breathing space to work out policy choices. Another nation, undergoing similar problems, might be met with more skepticism, resulting in a sell-off by foreign investors, then a currency collapse and panic that would make conditions even worse. Think of the experience of nations like Chile or Argentina, for instance, when financial crises have hit in the past. At the first sign of trouble, investors dumped their investments and fled, leading to a collapse in the currency, soaring interest rates, and a fierce economic decline.

But the single biggest economic benefit derived from the integrity of the Federal Reserve is the ability of the United States to borrow extremely cheaply. By maintaining the credibility of the nation, the Federal Reserve has enhanced the ability of the United States to borrow money readily from foreigners, directly financing the country's economic growth and wealth creation over decades. Without the ability of the nation to borrow freely from abroad, the U.S. economy would look very different today.

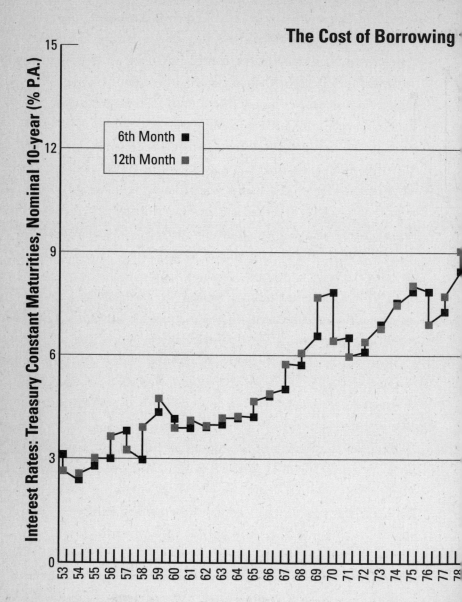

The Cost of Borrowing

Source: Moody's Economy.com

## United States 1953 to 2008

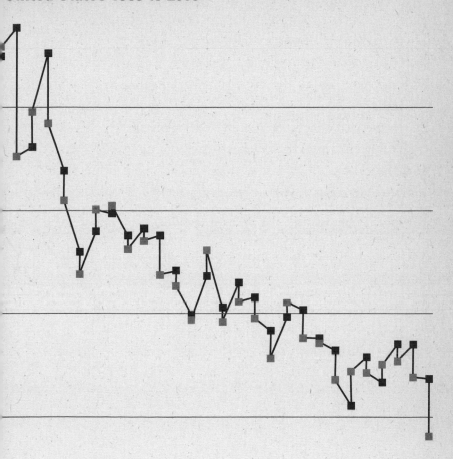

June & December – 1953 to 2008

Think for a moment what would happen if foreign investors stopped lending money to the United States. The initial effect would be a collapse of the dollar and financial markets. Longer term, economic growth would suffer as the nation slowly paid back the money it owed. Americans would have to be taxed more and at the same time have to save much more. Interest rates would rise steeply. The result would certainly be greatly reduced consumption and slower growth.

Ultimately, then, the readiness and willingness of the rest of the world to do business with Americans over time has become an enormous source of prosperity for the nation. The integrity built up at the Federal Reserve has been a critical factor in achieving that. Paying attention to the details of integrity isn't just something that's nice to do. It's good economics.

## CHAPTER FIVE

# Trusted Brands

. . . . . . . . . . . . . . . . . . . . . . . . . . . . . .

Sakichi Toyoda grew up in late 1800s Japan in a remote farming community outside of Nagoya. Toyoda trained as a carpenter but was fascinated by inventions. At the time, weaving was an essential part of every household, and the government encouraged the industry as a way to promote growth and lift families out of poverty. Mothers and grandmothers taught girls how to weave. Handwoven textiles were a critical focus of everyday life. But the work was often difficult, time-consuming, and produced imperfect results. Toyoda saw firsthand how hard weaving was, and believing he could make a more efficient loom, he began to experiment. It soon occurred to Toyoda that an automated loom was the answer, and in 1896 he invented Japan's first steam-powered loom.

Toyoda thought deeply about his new invention and wasn't satisfied. The steam-powered loom was easier to use and more efficient, but it still produced imperfect fabrics. One of the problems with weaving was the prevalence of defects in the fabric. If one thread snapped it could create a run, ruining a whole bolt of cloth. Most of the time, the weaver wouldn't even know a run had occurred and would continue to weave. The defect would essentially be built into the fabric and couldn't be corrected afterward. Toyoda considered the problem and invented a loom that automatically stopped whenever a single thread broke. The loom could then be reset and there would be no run in the fabric. Toyoda's "foolproof" loom was revolutionary. Not only was it laborsaving, but it produced higher-quality fabric as well.

In the 1920s, Toyoda established Toyoda Automatic Loom Works. A decade later, he sold the patent rights to his "foolproof" loom to a British company for one hundred thousand pounds, a considerable sum at the time. With that money he encouraged his son, Kiichiro, to start a new division within the company to make automobiles. In 1937, seven years after Sakichi Toyoda's death, that division became Toyota Motor Company.

From its humble beginnings in the Japanese countryside, Toyota has grown into a global powerhouse. At the end of 2008, the Japanese car manufacturer overtook General Motors as the biggest automaker in the world. It was a remarkable achievement. GM had dominated the global car industry for close to eighty years with no real peer and the entrenched commercial advantages of a market leader. Now that era is over. What's more, GM looks unlikely to unseat Toyota anytime soon, as it struggles to recover from bankruptcy. A careful, steady, and relentless focus on building better cars year after year has turned Toyota into the number one automotive brand in the world. It's a bit like the story of David and Goliath. Only in this story, David doesn't make a lucky hit. He eventually outgrows Goliath, an incredible feat of determination and hard work. So how did Toyota do it?

## Toyota Delivers on a Promise

IN THE BUSINESS world, Toyota is among the most closely watched and widely studied companies. Entire consulting firms are devoted to helping companies emulate the way Toyota does business. Its manufacturing processes have been dissected and copied by its rivals, its design and engineering are closely followed, and its philosophy and business practices have been the source of many textbooks. Out of all this effort to understand and replicate Toyota's success, the experts agree that what sets the company apart from its competitors is a relentless focus on quality. Toyota quality has become the gold standard for what a car should deliver to customers.

The reason quality has been so important to Toyota's success is not that quality is the most important ingredient consumers want in cars—that may or may not be the case—but because Toyota said it would deliver quality to customers and then kept its word. At times, that meant going to extraordinary lengths to ensure that quality was achieved. But by keeping its promise—that is, by acting with integrity—Toyota has built an enviable bond of trust with its customers.

That bond of trust has become extremely valuable. Experts in marketing and product development speak in terms of the brand. A brand isn't a catchy name or a symbol. It actually exists in the heads of consumers. Brands are perceptions about promises a company makes regarding its product or service and the ability to deliver on that promise. In effect, a brand is the way a company communicates its integrity to the marketplace. If a company doesn't follow through on its promise, its sales

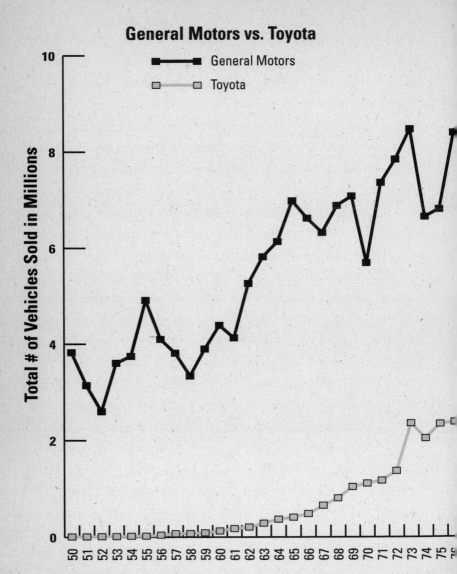

**General Motors vs. Toyota**

Source: General Motors and Toyota

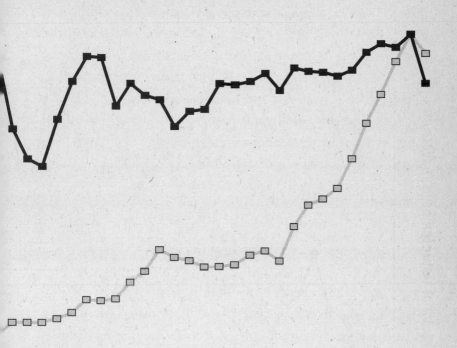

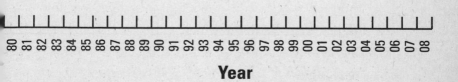

**Year**

will surely suffer. If it does follow through, it creates repeat opportunities to sell. A brand is stored-up integrity.

In Toyota's case, focusing on quality built its brand and delivered enormous financial rewards. It's a powerful lesson for anyone in the corporate world. Too often in business, the pressure to make money can be overwhelming, and integrity is seen as a cost. In practice, though, that thinking can lead to bad business strategies and decisions that eventually hurt a business. The story of Toyota's success is a story with a moral: integrity is an investment that offers substantial financial rewards. Toyota, after all, didn't build any old business selling cars. It built the biggest car business in the world.

## Toyota Quality

QUALITY MEANS DIFFERENT things to different people. Cloth is a good example of this. Couture clothing is considered to have high quality even though the fabrics used may not be durable or the style lasting. At the same time, jeans from the mall may deliver high quality on the basis that they are cheap and they last. The key to quality is delivering on a promise. In the marketplace, quality is integrity.

At Toyota, quality encompasses several different aspects of a vehicle: things like how well everything fits together, how good the finishes are, whether a vehicle is free of defects, and whether it is reliable.

Most companies offer some kind of quality assurance about their product or service. The difference for Toyota is that quality isn't a pledge or a throwaway line in its mission statement; it's a way of operating. Professor Jeffrey Liker, a leading expert on Toyota, explains it this way: "Quality has been designed in and built into every step of the process from understanding what the customer wants, to designing the look of the car, to the detailed engineering of every part of the car, to working with suppliers, to preparing tools and dies with high precision, to preparing the manufacturing plant and all the equipment, and to training and motivating the workforce to be passionate about quality." At Toyota, quality is a way of life.

When experts describe Toyota's "relentless" focus on quality, they mean that the company is committed to delivering quality no matter what the short-term cost may be to the firm or to its shareholders. In essence, it's a deep commitment to look after the customer and a philosophy that if you do, profits will follow. What Toyota is really saying is that quality, or integrity, is an investment.

Shotaro Kamiya, a highly respected executive at Toyota in the 1930s, captured the idea when he said: "The priority in receiving benefits from automobile sales should be in the order of the customer, then the car dealer, and, lastly, the maker. This attitude is the best approach in winning the trust of customers and dealers and ultimately brings growth to the manufacturer." What Toyota recognized from the outset was that its most important relationship was with customers. If the company acted with integrity, it would build a relationship of trust with its customers that would bring an economic payoff.

## Building in Success

SAKICHI TOYODA DID more than provide the funds that gave Toyota its start. He planted the seed of the company's success. Toyota incorporated Sakichi Toyoda's idea of building quality into the production process, and to this day that approach sets it apart from competitors. Over time that approach has evolved and become much more sophisticated, but the basic principle remains the same: build in systems to detect defects and correct mistakes as they are discovered.

On the factory floor that means a number of things. Machines have devices installed that detect abnormalities and automatically stop if there is a problem. The team can immediately identify the problem and correct the mistake, allowing production to continue.

Workers on the assembly line are expected and encouraged to detect problems. Every team member has the responsibility to stop the line each time they see something that is not standard. When they do, they can push a button that lights up at their station to alert their leader or pull a cord that plays music. At that point, the team may have several minutes to identify the error and fix it before the entire production line shuts down. By trying to openly identify problems and solve them as they appear, Toyota focuses on getting quality right the first time.

As a result, the factory floor at a Toyota plant looks very different from other manufacturing plants. Production lines tend to be set up in a U shape so that the beginning of the line and the end are next to each other. This facilitates communication, reduces unnecessary movement, and enables greater flexibility between production workers. Production lines also have visual displays everywhere indicating what and what not to do. Pull cords are in plain sight, and there are displays that immediately indicate where a problem has developed. The production lines themselves are simplified and clear of extra parts, containers, or parts-handling equipment. Nearby an Obeya, or big room, displays all the quality indicators and allows production teams to meet and review the results from that day.

Over time, manufacturers in the United States and elsewhere have tried to copy Toyota's method of building quality into the production process. For many it hasn't been an easy change. American-style mass production has tended to emphasize quantity over quality. Stopping an assembly line was discouraged. If defects were noticed, the product was typically set aside to be repaired later. That meant that some problems were never solved, and defects were built into the product.

## A Culture of Quality

TOYOTA'S LIGHTS AND music wouldn't add up to much without a culture that gets people to work together and trust each other. At Toyota, senior executives believe that quality is everyone's responsibility. On a regular basis, each team sets aside time to meet and discuss ways of making improvements in its area. These meetings, known as quality circles, are part of the underlying philosophy of the firm known as "continuous improvement," or *kaizen*. By trusting and respecting its employees,

Toyota has instilled respect for the customer and a commitment to provide value to anyone who buys a Toyota car.

Professor Liker describes Toyota's workforce as having an intense commitment to integrity:

> *Throughout my visits to Toyota in Japan and the United States, in engineering, purchasing, and manufacturing, one theme stands out. Every person I talked with has a sense of purpose greater than earning a paycheck. They feel a greater sense of mission for the company and can distinguish right from wrong with regard to that mission. They have learned the Toyota Way from their Japanese sensei (mentors) and the message is consistent: Do the right thing for the company, its employees, the customer, and society as a whole. Toyota's strong sense of mission and commitment to its customers, employees, and society is the foundation for all the other principles and the missing ingredient in most companies trying to emulate Toyota.*

## How Toyota Deals with Quality Problems

TOYOTA PRIDES ITSELF on creating lasting customer satisfaction. Its goal is to create loyalty, so that once customers buy a Toyota vehicle they are so satisfied with their experience they will never buy another brand again. In other words, Toyota wants to build a relationship with the customer for life.

That hasn't always gone smoothly. In 2005, the Big Three carmakers in the United States—General Motors, Ford, and

Chrysler—began to gloat. For the first time, Toyota was coming under pressure for quality problems. In that year alone, Toyota recalled more vehicles than it actually sold. Toyota's management was shocked. The firm quickly investigated where the problems were coming from and instituted a series of changes. The following year, the number of vehicles recalled was greatly reduced. By the end of 2008, the number of recalls in the United States was one-sixth of 2005 levels.

But what happens when something goes wrong at Toyota? Sometime at the beginning of 2008, Toyota discovered a problem with certain models of its Tacoma trucks. It found out that the frames of 1995 to 2000 model trucks were corroding from the inside out. Primarily, the company discovered, this occurred in trucks driven in areas where salt was used during the winter months to keep the roads clear.

After investigating the problem, Toyota judged it would not be able to fix the frames quickly and made an unusual decision: it would buy back the trucks from its customers. In March, just three months after the problems were discovered, Toyota launched a Tacoma truck customer support program. It offered to buy back 1995- to 2000-model trucks for one and a half times what they were deemed to be worth in the *Kelley Blue Book* (a widely used industry and consumer resource for estimating the value of a used vehicle). If a customer plugged in the age, model, and features of his Tacoma truck in the *Kelley Blue Book* and found it was worth ten thousand dollars, Toyota bought it back for fifteen thousand. In all, 813,000 vehicles were eligible for the program.

By industry standards, Toyota's buyback initiative was

highly unusual. In some cases the trucks were thirteen years old, ten years out of warranty. Many manufacturers would have washed their hands of the problem after such a long period of time. Yet Toyota was focused on giving its customers a good experience even after thirteen years. It wasn't calculating the minimum necessary to make things right with the customer again. Probably some form of rebate would have worked to deflect customer anger. But Toyota went above and beyond the minimum required.

In response, Toyota discovered that the reaction of its customers was very positive. More than a few of those truck owners who took part in the program took their check and immediately went to a Toyota dealer to buy another vehicle.

## The Payoff

THERE ARE MANY examples like the Tacoma truck story that show the lengths to which Toyota will go to build customer relationships. Over the years, that attitude has produced a substantial payoff for the company and its shareholders, employees, and business partners.

In the United States, Toyota's growth has been exceptional, especially given the dominant position of the Big Three automakers. It began operation of its American subsidiary in 1957 by importing Japanese cars. By the end of 2008 it had sales, manufacturing, R&D, and engineering operations across the nation and a total of eleven assembly plants.

In 1983, when Toyota started keeping track of data in the

United States, it employed 2,208 people. By 2008, it employed 36,000. In the ten years to 2008, Toyota went from selling 1.2 million vehicles a year in the United States to 2.6 million.

Globally, Toyota is considered the greatest manufacturer in the world. It is the most efficient and most popular automotive brand. Its worldwide sales grew from 6.7 million vehicles in 2003 to almost 9 million by 2008.

Toyota is in a solid position to weather the bleak global economic conditions that developed toward the end of 2008. Still, the going will be tough and the challenges are unprecedented. Car sales in the United States in the last half of 2008 virtually halved. Carmakers worldwide expect a new, sharply lower level of annual sales, as consumers adjust to tough conditions by keeping their vehicles far longer. For instance, it was commonplace for many Americans to buy a new car every three years or so prior to the precipitous economic slowdown.

By the beginning of 2009, carmakers were scrambling to adjust to the new economic environment. The once mighty GM was bankrupt and even after receiving an infusion of billions of dollars from the government to stay afloat, it was questionable whether the carmaker would make it through another year. Toyota, on the other hand, while experiencing its worst year for decades, was adjusting to the global collapse in demand for cars by delaying plant openings, scheduling changes in production, cutting costs, and investing strategically.

There's an important lesson in the diverging fates of Toyota and GM. Even before the economic downturn hit the global car market with enormous ferocity, GM was struggling. It had bet heavily on large and powerful cars like SUVs that captured

## J. D. Power and Associates
## 2009 Vehicle Dependability Study (VDS)

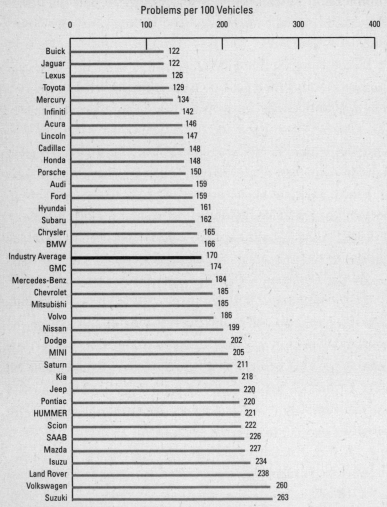

### 2009 Nameplate Ranking*

Problems per 100 Vehicles

| Nameplate | Problems per 100 Vehicles |
|---|---|
| Buick | 122 |
| Jaguar | 122 |
| Lexus | 126 |
| Toyota | 129 |
| Mercury | 134 |
| Infiniti | 142 |
| Acura | 146 |
| Lincoln | 147 |
| Cadillac | 148 |
| Honda | 148 |
| Porsche | 150 |
| Audi | 159 |
| Ford | 159 |
| Hyundai | 161 |
| Subaru | 162 |
| Chrysler | 165 |
| BMW | 166 |
| Industry Average | 170 |
| GMC | 174 |
| Mercedes-Benz | 184 |
| Chevrolet | 185 |
| Mitsubishi | 185 |
| Volvo | 186 |
| Nissan | 199 |
| Dodge | 202 |
| MINI | 205 |
| Saturn | 211 |
| Kia | 218 |
| Jeep | 220 |
| Pontiac | 220 |
| HUMMER | 221 |
| Scion | 222 |
| SAAB | 226 |
| Mazda | 227 |
| Isuzu | 234 |
| Land Rover | 238 |
| Volkswagen | 260 |
| Suzuki | 263 |

Source: J. D. Power and Associates 2009 Vehicle Dependability Study

*Rankings are based on numerical scores and not necessarily on statistical significance.

the imagination of Americans in an era of bigness but suddenly fell out of favor when oil prices skyrocketed. In essence, GM and the other U.S. car companies have tended toward gimmicks to sell cars—things that will get people's attention like size, powerful engines, zero-percent financing—anything to make a sale.

Toyota, on the other hand, took a more straightforward approach. It said, "We'll sell you a car that does what you expect it to do." And Toyota has delivered on its promise consistently, year after year.

While plenty of car buyers have preferred flash to quality over the years, the single biggest thing that U.S. automakers underestimated was the destructive potential of defects.

When a car is sold with defects, it communicates dishonesty, and over time a reputation of dishonesty is hard to shake. On the other hand, a car sold without defects builds trust and creates a loyal customer base.

The crucial point is that the Big Three didn't appreciate how damaging it was to sell cars with defects while at the same time continuing to claim they were focused on quality. Over time, it destroyed the bond of trust with customers. So while U.S. carmakers focused on selling excitement, they did not focus on selling trust. And they've paid a heavy price in terms of customer loyalty and profitability.

## Building a Brand, Investing in Integrity, and Reaping the Rewards

Damaging the bond of trust with customers destroys a brand and ultimately eviscerates the ability of a company to generate wealth.

Trust is one of the most valuable commodities in the marketplace. To understand why, think of it in terms of the value of a brand. When customers buy Coca-Cola, for instance, they know exactly what they're getting: sugar and caffeine that create a buzz, the same taste every time, attractive and convenient packaging, imagery of happy people drinking Coke, and the ability to reach for a Coke wherever they may be. If customers expect all that but get something less, don't count on them to buy the product again.

Imagery and advertising can enhance and shape a brand, but in the end, if there's no substance behind the imagery, the brand will flop. That's because a brand is really a shorthand way of communicating trustworthiness to millions of extremely diverse people and cultures. It doesn't matter if a firm has all the integrity in the world if people don't know that or don't believe it. There has to be an efficient way to communicate that integrity and get paid for it. That's the clever function of a brand.

Once a firm has a reputation for integrity, it makes selling much easier. It also enhances a firm's ability to charge what it wants for its product. Unlike a commodity, a brand is something distinctive. It is a little monopoly where customers are willing to pay a bit more for something they trust. And trusted brands can help companies launch new product lines. Think of Diet Coke, for instance. Brands are an achievement of integrity. They are about companies delivering what they say they will deliver.

Successful brands—and that means successful companies—tend to share a common quality. They think long and hard about the customer and the experience the customer is getting from the product or service. Toyota, for example, is not spending its time calculating how to get paid. It's thinking about what has to be done to really satisfy the customer, even if that doesn't mean getting paid on day one. And that often means delivering something that wasn't asked for but will be appreciated. Over time, customers can tell when they are looked after.

In the short term, companies face enormous pressure to cut corners and save money or exploit trust to make money. Often it's easy to justify these decisions based on the letter of the law. As long as I'm not breaking the law, the thinking goes, then it doesn't matter what I do. That type of thinking, though, has proved to be an abject failure. Remember subprime lending? While lending to people unlikely to meet their mortgage payments wasn't illegal, it didn't prove to be a good long-term strategy either.

The key question for any product or service should be this: does this product create lasting value for the customer? Of course, asking that question is standard practice in business. What may be less common is answering it honestly.

It's easy to suggest that companies need to focus on the long term, but the commercial reality is that both the short term and the long term are important. One way through the maze of competing interests is to understand how short-term decisions affect the long term. For instance, if selling a particular product in the short term hurts a firm's ability to sell in the future, then that product is almost never worth selling. Sacrificing the long term for the short term is not a viable strategy.

But when firms view integrity as a cost, it can mean putting their short-term interests ahead of the long term. And frequently that can lead to trouble. Integrity is the goose that lays the golden eggs. If you nurture and protect it, the goose will keep laying golden eggs. But if you starve it or try to get all the eggs at once, you'll have nothing left for the future.

As the corporate world grapples with the extent of the economic downturn, there will be pressure to go back to basics. What that really means is doing what works—focusing on the customer, creating value, and acting with integrity. They're the same thing. Investing in integrity isn't a get-rich-quick scheme. But it is a proven way to build profitable and successful companies.

## CHAPTER SIX

# Trusting Customers

. . . . . . . . . . . . . . . . . . . . . . . . . . . . . .

L eon Leonwood Bean had a passion for the outdoors. In 1911, after a long hunting trip, he returned home with a rather unpleasant feeling. His feet were miserably wet and cold. He imagined how satisfying it would be to have a hunting shoe that kept his feet warm and dry when he was deep in the Maine woods. Bean was about forty years old at the time and worked as the manager of his brother's shoe store in Freeport, Maine. He searched for a shoe that might meet his needs but was completely unsatisfied with what he found. Bean decided to make his own hunting shoe and approached a local cobbler to help. The shoe was essentially made by sewing rugged leather uppers to waterproof rubber bottoms. Excited by the prospect of his new hunting shoe, Bean began to think about how he could get other hunters to try it. In 1912, he came across a mailing list of nonresident Maine hunting license holders, and he had an idea. He would create a flyer explaining his revolutionary new product and send it out to everyone on the list. In the flyer he made a bold statement: "You cannot expect success hunting deer or moose if your feet are not properly dressed. The Maine Hunting Shoe is designed by a hunter who has tramped the Maine woods for the last 18 years. We guarantee them to give perfect satisfaction in every way."

That guarantee almost ended Bean's business before it got started. Bean received one hundred orders for his Maine Hunting Shoe and was pleased with the initial response. But it turned out there was a defect in his product. Upon wearing, the sole separated from the tops of the shoes. Out of the first one hundred pairs of shoes that Bean sold, ninety pairs were returned. True to his word, Bean borrowed money to return the payment for all ninety pairs of shoes. It was a humbling lesson, but it didn't stop him. Bean went about fixing the problem and sent out more flyers. That was the beginning of L.L.Bean, one of America's most successful family businesses and a household name.

For close to a century, L.L.Bean has maintained its 100 percent guarantee without altering its commitment in any way. No matter how long a customer has worn or used a product, no matter what the problem is, any L.L.Bean product can be returned for a full refund at any time. It's worth thinking about what that guarantee means for a moment. No matter whether L.L.Bean agrees with the customer or not, it's the customer's opinion that counts. And it reflects a core value that seems somewhat clichéd today but has been around for a very long time: "The customer is always right." At the heart of that value and of L.L.Bean's commitment to the customer is trust. The company trusts the customer to behave fairly.

L.L.Bean's unlimited return policy sets it apart from many other retailers. Lands' End, a successful competitor to L.L.Bean, has mimicked the guarantee. By far the more typical policy for retailers is to limit returns to within thirty to ninety days of a purchase, and it's easy to find stores that have restrictions on returns that amount to some form of "gotcha" for consumers. Frequently stores won't consider a return without a receipt, and often the sales tags must remain intact. Then there are sale items, for which many retailers refuse any refund at all. What's more, even within the same chain, stores may have different return policies and at different times of the year. Nowadays, big stores like Wal-Mart, Home Depot, and Barnes and Noble are even using software to identify which customers are returning items frequently, so that the stores can refuse returns at their discretion.

So is L.L.Bean's policy just a marketing stunt? Or is it a fundamentally different and valuable approach to business?

It takes some effort to provide customers with unlimited returns. For starters, a company needs to employ and train a first-class customer support staff so that it can handle returns, questions, and problems in a friendly, helpful, and efficient manner. And the company's response needs to be consistent, whether the customer is making an outrageous claim or not. A company that guarantees its products may be inviting consumers to take it on in some extreme way, in essence to test the company's limits.

Most companies that offer unlimited guarantees have a tale or two to tell about outrageous customer behavior. Lands'

End has even turned those episodes to its own advantage and promotes the lengths it goes to in order to honor its commitment to the customer. On its Web site, Lands' End explains how customers have tested its policy over the years and offers an example. In its 1984 holiday catalog, Lands' End featured an original London taxi on the cover. A lady from Kansas contacted the company to purchase the taxi for her car-collecting husband. At the time, she agreed on a price of nineteen thousand dollars, and the sale was made. More than ten years later, her husband contacted Lands' End and asked for his money back. Lands' End obliged and used the incident to drive home its point: absolutely everything the company sells comes with an unconditional guarantee.

Over the years, L.L.Bean has found that customers who try to take advantage of its unlimited return policy in an unfair way are by far the minority. Most people deal honestly with the company, and both sides have benefited. Customers are truly satisfied with the products they buy, and the company experiences repeat business. The point is that when L.L.Bean, Lands' End, or anyone with an unlimited return policy essentially says that they trust you, the customer, you understand that trust and respond favorably. Henry Stimson, the American secretary of war during World War II, famously said, "The only way to make a man trustworthy is to trust him." Just think about how it feels to be trusted. It brings a feeling of being valued and respected. That can build a commercial relationship and bring economic rewards.

In business, a relationship of trust isn't just one-sided. Business is based not only on what a company does but on what customers do. Understanding what companies like Toyota have done to win consumers' trust is one side of the coin. Trusting the customer is the other. Together, the two sides create value. If one side does something to destroy the bond of trust, it can ruin the relationship. Often, though, business executives can forget to trust the customer, and instead assume the worst in people. That may lead to bad business practices like putting onerous restrictions on returns or not standing by the quality of products once they are sold for fear that the company will be exploited.

All businesses have to trust their customers to some extent. When offering a product or service for sale, sellers depend on customers not to complain without reason, abuse return policies, bad-mouth the product unfairly, or mistreat the product. Think back to dairy farmers for a moment. They trust milk drinkers to treat milk appropriately: not to keep it out of the fridge or consume it past the use-by date. If consumers did mistreat milk, they might end up sick that might and create a backlash against milk.

Both sides in a successful commercial relationship have something at stake—the customer genuinely wants the business to succeed in order to keep getting the same product or service, and the business wants the customer to have a good experience to get repeat business. Some companies like L.L.Bean have long recognized the value of trusting the customer and communicating that trust. Not only does L.L.Bean offer unlimited returns, it demonstrates its trust in other ways too, some of them symbolic. For instance, it never locks its flagship store in Freeport. As in L.L.Bean's case, by understanding the value of trusting customers, companies can unlock significant financial rewards. It just may represent one of the biggest untapped sources of wealth out there today.

• • • • • • • • • • • • • • • • • • • • • • • • • • • • • • • • • • • • • • •

## Who Provides the Best Customer Service?

### Customer Service Rankings

| Rank | Overall BEST | Rank | Overall BEST |
|------|--------------|------|--------------|
| 1 | L.L.Bean | 23 | ACE Hardware |
| 2 | Overstock.com | 24 | Old Navy |
| 3 | Zappos | 25 | Target |
| 4 | Amazon | 26 | Apple |
| 5 | Lands' End | 27 | Victoria's Secret |
| 6 | Newegg | 28 | Dillard's |
| 7 | J.C. Penney | 29 | Wegmans |
| 8 | QVC | 30 | Kroger |
| 9 | Coldwater Creek | 31 | Wal-Mart |
| 10 | Nordstrom | 32 | Lowe's |
| 11 | Cabela's | 33 | Publix |
| 12 | TigerDirect.com | 34 | Meijer |
| 13 | Lane Bryant | 35 | Costco |
| 14 | eBay | 36 | Kmart |
| 15 | Sears | 37 | Home Depot |
| 16 | HSN | 38 | Staples |
| 17 | Best Buy | 39 | Safeway |
| 18 | Kohl's | 40 | Walgreens |
| 19 | Macy's | 41 | Sam's Club |
| 20 | Radio Shack | 42 | Verizon |
| 21 | Belk | 43 | Dell |
| 22 | Circuit City | 44 | CVS |

Source: BIGresearch, Consumer Intentions and Actions (CIA) Survey, September 2008

• • • • • • • • • • • • • • • • • • • • • • • • • • • • • • • • • • • • • • •

## How L.L.Bean's Trust Has Paid Off

WHEN IT COMES to customer service, few other retailers consistently rate as high on consumer surveys as L.L.Bean.

For two years running, L.L.Bean was ranked number one in customer service by the National Retail Federation Foundation/American Express survey; number one among clothing catalog companies in the Brand Keys Customer Loyalty Index for the sixth consecutive year; number one "online leader" by *Women's Wear Daily*—and so on. It's been the same every year: if L.L.Bean is not number one, then it's up there among the leaders.

Industry observers believe that L.L.Bean's high standing with consumers has to do with its unlimited return policy. Customers know that if they buy a product and it doesn't meet their expectations, they'll have no problem getting what they want or getting their money back. It inspires confidence among consumers that the company is not out to get them but is genuinely on their side and wants them to have a good experience. And it shows that the company trusts its customers not to abuse the return policy but to use it to achieve genuine satisfaction with what they buy. Furthermore, customers believe in the products because the company itself is prepared to stand by what it makes. In a sense, L.L.Bean trusts in the integrity of what it makes. When Bean sold his first one hundred pairs of shoes, he made a critical error by not testing his product first. After his experience with an initial defect, he made a point of personally testing all his products and making sure he was satisfied too.

L.L.Bean has found from customer comments that the guarantee contributes to customer loyalty. Over the years, the company has moved from making the Maine Hunting Shoe to making over twenty thousand products. While Bean started with hunting, camping, and fishing apparel and equipment, today the company sells men's, women's, and children's fashions, all types of clothes and shoes for the outdoors, as well as equipment for outdoor activities and home furnishings.

In addition to customer loyalty, L.L.Bean believes its unlimited return policy helps it to understand what customers want and be responsive to their needs. The company tracks returns very carefully to identify trends and potential product problems, such as sizing, fit, and durability. This enables the company to make design adjustments or changes in the materials used. Over the years, it's been a key source of creating products that satisfy the customer.

The payoff has been growing sales and business expansion both in the United States and abroad for close to a century. In 1937, sales passed the $1 million mark. By 1961, sales had passed $2 million. In 2008, L.L.Bean's sales stood at $1.5 billion. Today the company employs fifty-four hundred people year-round and twelve thousand during the winter holiday season. It has gone from one basic catalog back at the beginning of the business to fifty-five catalogs distributed in the United States and one hundred sixty other countries. In 2008, a total of nearly 13 million customers placed orders with L.L.Bean. And L.L.Bean trusts every single one of them.

## Trusting Somebody Else's Customer

IN HER NINETIES, Vieve Gore could still get tears in her eyes when she recounted the early days of her husband's business endeavors. It was the late 1950s and Bill Gore had left a perfectly good job as an engineer with DuPont to try his hand at making his own products. Working from the couples' home in Newark, Delaware, Bill spent hours in the basement or out on the lawn making wire cables by hand. But the thing that really upset Vieve was when she came home one day to find that many of her pots and pans had been ruined in one of Bill's experiments. At the time, Vieve had no idea how successful her husband, and later her son, would be. Starting with insulated wire and cable, which Bill sold to the growing aerospace and computer industries, W. L. Gore and Associates has become one of the top two hundred privately owned companies in the United States. Today, with revenues of more than $2 billion, Gore sells a range of consumer and industrial products as well as medical devices.

If you buy any quality outdoor jacket today, whether the brand is North Face or any other big name, there's a good chance it will be made with GORE-TEX fabric. Invented in the 1970s, the fabric was a revolutionary product that was both waterproof and breathable and became the company's best-known brand. The success of GORE-TEX fabric is an intriguing story about how a single business decision created a successful product and ultimately a diversified business. That decision amounted to trusting customers. But Gore didn't just decide to trust its own customers. It created a highly profitable business by trusting somebody else's customers.

It all began in the 1980s when Gore was wondering how to capture the imagination of consumers with its fabric. By 1982, GORE-TEX had established a good reputation among manufacturers, but there didn't seem to be any buzz from people actually using the end product. Gore turned to the mountaineering community and in essence began a conversation with end users that has grown over decades.

Initially the company got more than it bargained for. As Gore reached out to consumers of outdoor wear, GORE-TEX began to be the name most associated with jackets, more so than the actual retail brand name. The company encouraged consumers to call its number if they experienced any problems with the fabric. So when consumers found that their jackets leaked, they started calling Gore directly. Gore patiently told customers that the problem wasn't its fabric but the jacket design, so they should really talk to the jacket manufacturer. Yet the calls kept coming. If Gore's fabric was waterproof, consumers thought that their jackets should be waterproof too. It was a development that could have ended the business. Bob Gore, son of Vieve and Bill, who was in charge of the company at the time, realized it was a critical moment.

Gore asked consumers to send in their jackets and the company studied the problem. What they found was shocking. Gore quickly discovered that about 80 percent of the problems were not its fault. The fabric itself did what Gore said it would do until a single stitch was sewn. As soon as a needle was inserted into the fabric, it created the potential for leakage. It might not have been Gore's fault, but it was certainly Gore's problem if it wanted a thriving fabrics business.

First, Gore began experimenting with new technology to make sure the seams of jackets could be sealed—a process known as seamseal. Next, it made a single business decision that many executives believe was the defining moment for the company. Gore guaranteed that GORE-TEX would keep consumers dry, no matter what. It was 1989, and Gore rolled out its "Guaranteed to Keep You Dry" promise to the amazement of many other companies. It was the first time that a component supplier was essentially guaranteeing the end product. Companies like Intel watched closely.

Gore explained its guarantee like this: There was no time limit on customer satisfaction. If a customer wasn't completely satisfied with the product, Gore would refund, replace, or repair it. It was a big vote of trust in somebody else's customer. A buyer of a North Face jacket could potentially abuse the product but expect Gore, the fabric maker, to replace it. But if Gore was to guarantee the end product, it needed to get manufacturers on board too. And that turned out to be quite a challenge.

Essentially, Gore told its customers, major garment manufacturers, that if they wanted to use GORE-TEX they had to change the way they designed and made their products. At first, the reaction wasn't promising. Many manufacturers were indignant, and some simply walked away. Gore patiently explained to those who were willing to talk that their jackets needed a new, better design. The company brought key executives to its plant and showed how their jackets performed in a rain room for thirty minutes. For some, it was evidence they were prepared to act on. Gore licensed its trademark to its manufacturing partners in return for being able to set quality standards in manufacturing.

In the first three years, the decision actually cost Gore business. By the mid-1990s, though, Gore found its fabrics business starting to take off. By that time the outdoor market was growing rapidly, and consumers were impressed with Gore's "Guaranteed to Keep You Dry" promise. Gore found that customers were loyal to its products and had a high repurchase rate. But Gore's promise of "Guaranteed to Keep You Dry" was critical to the growth of its other business units as well. The goodwill generated by the GORE-TEX label spilled over into other areas where manufacturers understood and were impressed that Gore really did stand behind its products. It has enabled the company to grow into such diverse areas as medical devices, which have been extremely profitable in recent years and depend on reputations for high-quality products. Gore's decision to guarantee its fabrics wasn't easy or without daunting challenges, yet everyone within the company agrees that it was the best thing they ever did.

## Pay What You Want

ON OCTOBER 10, 2007, British alternative rock group Radiohead created a sensation around the world. After six successful albums with the EMI record label, the band decided to do something radical. So radical, in fact, that it may one day end up transforming the music business. Instead of releasing their seventh album on a record label, Radiohead released *In Rainbows* on their own Web site as a download. But the real shock was caused by a simple, seemingly innocuous phrase next to the download button: "It's up to you." Radiohead had decided fans could pay what they wanted for the album.

The music industry quickly rushed to point out that only those bands with a substantial following could hope to follow Radiohead's lead, and even then they probably wouldn't make any money. And yet in the weeks that followed, Radiohead found that 2 million fans downloaded the album. While some paid nothing, most fans did pay, and according to the band, the album was profitable. Better yet, *In Rainbows* received critical acclaim and enhanced the band's popularity.

Radiohead's pay-what-you-want album was an experiment. Since then other musicians have been flirting with the same pricing model. Hip-hop singer Niggy Tardust and comedian Steve Hofstetter have both tried pay-what-you-want albums. When Hofstetter released *The Dark Side of the Room*, he found that on average a fan paid six dollars for the download. According to record industry experts, at that price the album could be profitable.

It's not just the music industry that's experimenting with pay-what-you-want pricing models. Small software operators on the Web have been trying it out, as well as restaurants around the world. In cities like Vienna, Berlin, Seattle, Melbourne, and Denver, diners can sit down and experience a full-course meal and then simply decide what that meal was worth. It's something that New York museums have been doing for some time. Visit the Metropolitan Museum of Art or the American Museum of Natural History and you'll see a posted entry fee that most visitors gladly pay. But look closely and you'll find that the fee is merely "suggested," a recommendation or a guideline, something that savvy New Yorkers have long understood. The entrance fee to those world-class museums is, in fact, up to you.

What makes pay-what-you-want pricing so intriguing is that the service or product provider expects the customer not only to pay but to pay a fair price. Yet there's nothing at all requiring the customer to do that. It's based on pure trust. And most of the time it works. A group of researchers in Germany conducted experiments at restaurants and movies to see how much people paid when it was left to them to decide. They found that given the option to name any price for a lunch buffet, movie, or drink, consumers paid an average of 86 percent of the regular prices and always paid something. It's easy to imagine that a onetime customer might not feel like paying anything, and yet the researchers found that it didn't happen. Studying how repeat customers respond over time to pay-what-you-want models may shed light on how trust builds customer loyalty that has a financial payoff.

Consumers may also find that a pricing model based on users' discretion is a refreshing change from one that figures out clever ways of making you pay the maximum possible. Think of the airline industry, which has many different prices for seats on the same flight. If you need to travel on a certain flight, you probably find you are paying much more than the person sitting next to you, who bought at the last moment when the price of the air ticket was reduced to fill the seat. Pricing models that the airlines employ tend to make people feel that they're being pushed around and in the end destroy the bond of trust with the customer.

Still, pay-what-you-want businesses haven't found large-scale success yet. At least no one has figured out so far how to turn them into a scalable business. But it's not a fanciful idea. If you need proof, just look at tipping: it's based on the same idea and has worked for years. In the United States, at least, tipping is both widespread and an important economic behavior. And it's all about leaving payment up to the discretion of the customer.

Each day about one in ten Americans sits down to eat at a full-service restaurant. In a month, almost 60 percent of Americans will have gone out to enjoy a full-service meal. In a year, that amounts to around $27 billion in tips paid to the nation's 2 million or so waitstaff. In many cases, those waiters and waitresses might depend entirely on tips in order to get paid. And yet while it's customary to tip, there's no legal or binding requirement to do so.

Tipping is a powerful model for the service business. When it comes to dining, we all understand what the recommendation is for tipping—a standard 15 to 20 percent. Yet it's widely understood that you might pay more if you're very satisfied with your experience or less if you're not satisfied. Most of the time, people tend to pay the standard tip. It's interesting to think for a moment about why we actually follow through and pay a tip. After all, the service has already been provided; there's little more that can enhance a diner's experience after the bill is paid. But in a sense we've internalized the standard tip and feel as if we're cheating the waiter or waitress if we don't pay. In effect, we'd feel embarrassed or that we were letting somebody down. Especially when we know that the server may depend entirely on tips.

Restaurants aren't the only service providers that rely on tips. A large segment of the service industry does too. Think about all the people you may tip in the course of a day: hairdressers, barbers, bellhops, maids, parking attendants, beauticians, masseuses, washroom attendants, porters, taxi drivers, and delivery people. All those people trust that the person receiving the service will pay a fair price for their service.

Tipping offers a valuable insight for fledgling pay-what-you-want businesses. Why does it work? The reason is that we have developed standards for tipping—10 percent in taxis, 15 percent at hairdressers, and so on. People understand what the norm is and make decisions around that norm. They also understand why it is the norm. In the case of waitstaff, you know they are lucky to make the minimum wage and most depend on tips for their livelihood.

The lesson for the music industry is to develop a standard or recommended rate for an album that's downloaded from a Web site. It would also be important to help fans understand what's behind that price. How much goes directly to the artists? Where else does the money go? At what average price can the artist break even? If fans are armed with that information, they know what they should pay to support an artist they like and appreciate. If pay-what-you-want pricing models are to succeed, consumers need some guidance and then room to make up their own minds.

Business models that demonstrate trust in the customer have an exciting potential for growth. Most businesses today tend to ignore the issue or take it for granted. Of course, to actively trust the customer, a company first must make sure its own house is in order. You can't sell faulty or unreliable products or services and then expect the customer to treat you fairly. But when you do your best on behalf of the customers and then trust the customers to do their best on behalf of you, you can create something lasting and valuable. People have a deep need to be trusted. They value the trust of others, and in general what people value they will pay for. It boils down to what Dale Carnegie advised long ago: give the other person a fine reputation to live up to. On that simple principle a commercial empire can be built.

## CHAPTER SEVEN

# Trading on Your Word

..................................

The money never sleeps. Well before sunrise, the first person trickles in; then more follow. By 6:30 A.M. the trading floor at a big investment bank is buzzing. Less than an hour later, everyone has settled in to work. Tailored jackets are crushed over the backs of chairs, monogrammed cuffs are rolled up, computer screens are flickering, and phones rise off the hook. Traders parse through the events that took place overnight in Asian and European markets and focus on the day ahead.

Precisely at 9:30 A.M. trading officially begins. The buzz on the floor turns to a roar as the pace of activity instantly picks up. Hundreds of traders, salespeople, and their many assistants work side by side in a vast open space that allows each one to call or signal to a colleague from a hundred feet or so across the room. On the trading floor there's no personal space. Desks are a few feet apart, stacked with computer screens and monitors. Around twenty traders staff the bank's corporate bond desk. Each one specializes in a particular subset of companies, like industrials or financials.

A salesman calls over to the trader handling industrials at a desk nearby. The salesman has been e-mailing clients about a particular General Electric bond. Large companies, like GE, typically have dozens of different bonds in the marketplace at one time. In this case, the bond has a coupon of 5 percent and maturity of 2013. The salesman has a client interested in buying several million and he tells the trader to fill the order.

The trader sizes up the market, knows where he can get that quantity, and makes a bid. It's accepted and he calls back over to the salesman to let him know the trade is done. The salesman e-mails the client that the trade has been executed. It happens in minutes.

This is the $25 trillion bond market. In investment and commercial banks across the nation, government financial institutions like the Federal Reserve Bank of New York, and large money management firms like Fidelity, the scene is much the same. There's no formal exchange for bonds as there is for stocks. Here in the bond market, financial securities trade over the phone or electronically in the "over-the-counter" market. By far the vast majority of trading that occurs every day in financial markets in the United States is done in this way. And much of it depends on the spoken word.

## Integrity in a Single Trade

In that particular GE trade, the bonds are plain vanilla and probably trade more than a hundred times a day. As a result, everything happens almost automatically; execution of the trade and settlement are standard. Yet even this simple bond sale relies on a great deal of integrity. Without it, the trade wouldn't take place.

When the trader buys the bonds in the market, he has to trust that the person on the other end of the phone will deliver. He believes that the seller actually has the bonds and will hand them over at the agreed price and within the required time frame. At the same time, the seller trusts the trader to keep his word too. The trader has to deliver payment at the agreed time.

Traders appreciate the value of their reputation and try to protect it. A simple way they do that is by using taped phone lines. If a dispute does arise over a trade, traders can go back to the phone conversation and replay it. Misunderstandings are often quickly corrected once both parties recall what was agreed on.

When a trader says "done" on a trade, even if market conditions change in the interim and he's lost money, he's still going through with it. And that scenario happens all the time. A trader may lose money on a transaction but expects to make it up on others. He can't very well walk away from losing trades only to stand by winning ones.

What's more, that rule of keeping your word still holds true during tumultuous times in the market. Even when traders lose big, they still honor the trade. Whether they have the money to follow through and meet payments can be another matter. But the basic fact remains that very seldom does a trader try to walk away from a trade he's executed.

The client is trusted to follow through on the trade as well. The salesperson doesn't expect to report to the client that bonds are bought only to find that the client has changed his mind and backed out of the deal. Even though the actual trade may take only seconds, the settlement time is far longer. Three days is normal for a simple trade like the one involving the GE bonds to be completed. In that time, it's possible that one side or the other may regret the decision and want to cancel the trade. Yet that almost never happens.

A trader explains it this way: "In my sixteen years of trading in fixed income, I've found the vast majority of issues are due to misunderstandings. Only a handful of times do I remember someone saying I don't want to complete a trade. Typically, that's only going to happen if the counterparty is in real trouble and isn't thinking about the future. . . . Reputation and trust is sort of an entry requirement in the market. All market participants are assumed to go by 'your word is your bond.'"

## What's at Stake?

IT'S ASTOUNDING WHEN you consider how much money depends on the ability of traders to keep their word. Just in the bond market alone, close to $1 trillion trades on an average day. That's $1 trillion traded daily on the basis of somebody's word, around $250 trillion in a single year.

It's not just the bond market that trades on trust, though. The entire multitrillion-dollar world of trading does too. The sheer value of all financial assets traded on the basis of a promise, every minute, every day, year after year, is staggering.

In 2007, on all major stock, options, and futures exchanges in the United States, a total of $66 trillion worth of assets was traded. Out of that figure, by far the biggest exchanges were the New York Stock Exchange and the NASDAQ. Together they accounted for about half the total.

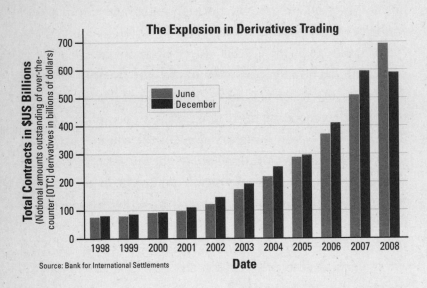

**The Explosion in Derivatives Trading**

Source: Bank for International Settlements

Add up the market value of trading in those major financial instruments in a year—$250 trillion for bonds, $66 trillion on exchanges, more for foreign exchange and derivatives—and you've got a pretty good indication of just how big the world of trading actually is: somewhere around $400 trillion each year.

While the U.S. economy stands at roughly $14 trillion, the market value of trading in a year could approach twenty-five times that. It amounts to a phenomenal sum of money riding on a trader's word.

## How Integrity Creates Efficiencies

WHEN TRANSACTIONS ARE done on a verbal basis and only later confirmed in writing, a person's word is an incredibly valuable asset. Integrity is the critical factor that allows traders to trade.

Think back to the GE bond trade for a moment. What is going through the trader's mind when he is in the market buying bonds?

The trader executes a standard trade in about twenty seconds. In that time, he's thinking about ten different things. For instance, he's asking: "Should I buy some of these bonds for myself?" "What's happening in the market that could affect this trade?" "What might the price do while I'm holding these bonds?" And so on go the thoughts. But the one thing the trader isn't thinking about is this: "Do I trust the guy on the other side of the trade?"

If the trader had to worry about whether the person on the other end of the phone would follow through on the deal, he literally couldn't function. In the twenty seconds he has to do the trade, he can't be thinking about whether he trusts the other person, only about what the market risks are.

When freed up to focus on market conditions and risk, the trader can be extremely efficient. A trade that normally takes twenty seconds might take far longer, perhaps even days, if the trader had to prove he was trustworthy and be reassured about the integrity of the person on the other side of the trade. Traders simply wouldn't do as much business.

The point is that we can do things far more cheaply and efficiently if we have a relationship of integrity and trust. Allowing traders to trade quickly over and over again makes capital markets amazingly efficient.

## How Those Efficiencies Create Wealth

IT'S EASY TO understand how integrity makes those traders better off, but what about the rest of us?

The great economic benefit of trading is that it allows money to flow freely in the economy. Whenever there's the slightest demand in the system, money flows quickly to meet that demand. Whenever there's the slightest supply of funds, money becomes available for investment. Trading then creates wealth in two ways: by putting people together and by doing that quickly and cheaply.

On one side are people with money: individuals, companies, governments, and nonprofits. On the other side are people who need money: consumers, home buyers, car buyers, companies, and governments. In the middle are the money managers, hedge funds, investment banks, commercial banks, and the like who match the needs of the two sides. While there are lots of complicated products involved, putting all the fancy footwork aside, trading provides a key function— it matches people who have money with those who need money and allows economic activity to flourish. If borrowers aren't matched to lenders, activity dependent on capital can't occur.

But it's not much use if it takes months for capital to flow from savers to those with pressing needs. It has to happen fast. That's where integrity comes in. Integrity and trust are crucial for decisions to be made quickly.

In a capitalist economy, the efficient allocation of capital is the single most important factor driving economic activity. And it all depends on integrity.

## What It's Worth

STOP TO THINK about the speed at which capital flows for a moment. What does that really mean?

Financial types call it liquidity. That means how readily an asset trades. The easier it is to trade an asset, the more liquid it is, and the more valuable that makes it. Liquidity makes things valuable.

You quickly see how valuable liquidity is when it disappears. During the 2008 panic, part of the problem in credit markets was a lack of liquidity. When the market for certain assets essentially dried up, no one could buy or sell, and those assets became effectively worthless for a time.

Financial experts assign a premium to assets based on liquidity: the liquidity premium. While experts may disagree over the exact size of the premium for stocks, it's generally considered to be around 30 percent. That means that if there were two identical companies and one was traded on the stock exchange while the other was not, the value of the company traded on the stock exchange would be 30 percent higher.

Using the liquidity premium, it's possible to derive a dollar value for what trading is actually worth. Take the NYSE, for instance. Since the entire market value of NYSE companies was roughly $9 trillion at the end of 2008, the value derived from NYSE trading would be 30 percent of that figure, or about $3 trillion. That means that trading is actually adding $3 trillion or so to the combined value of those companies. The global total for stock exchanges is even bigger, about $32 trillion at the end of 2008. That means that the value added from trading stocks on world markets may be around $10 trillion.

Integrity is worth trillions of dollars in relation to the stock market alone. Imagine how integrity multiplies value throughout the entire economy.

## Valuing Integrity Elsewhere

OF COURSE, TRADING is only one example of how integrity and trust create efficiencies and wealth. The same principle ripples throughout our modern economy. Perhaps the most significant innovation enabling an advanced consumer economy is the practice of brand marketing.

Brands, like Toyota, are an astonishingly efficient means of encapsulating a "promise" that the consumer can trust. The whole purpose of a brand is so consumers don't need to spend time thinking about which washing detergent to buy. They just look for the trademark they trust and buy it. And it's the same with business brands. Think of IBM or Cisco Systems. When firms need to buy computer equipment or software systems, a brand is a shorthand way of establishing trust.

One way to appreciate how much integrity is actually worth would be to add up the value of all the brands in the nation.

Some of the most valuable brands are thought to be Coca-Cola, which has been valued at $67 billion; IBM, with a brand value estimated at $59 billion; and Microsoft, also at $59 billion. Think of Amazon, American Express, McDonald's, Coke, Citibank, Google, and so on. There are thousands of brands around today, each ranging in value from a few million to tens of billions of dollars. Adding up the value of all the brands in the economy would certainly amount to trillions of dollars. One survey of the one hundred top global brands in 2008 put their combined value at $1.2 trillion.

# The Value of Brands

## Add it up: the top 100 global brands are worth a total of $1.2 trillion

| 2008 Rank | Brand | 2008 Brand Value ($ Millions) | Country of Ownership |
|:---:|:---:|:---:|:---:|
| 1 | Coca-Cola | 66,667.00 | U.S. |
| 2 | IBM | 59,031.00 | U.S. |
| 3 | Microsoft | 59,007.00 | U.S. |
| 4 | GE | 53,086.00 | U.S. |
| 5 | Nokia | 35,942.00 | Finland |
| 6 | Toyota | 34,050.00 | Japan |
| 7 | Intel | 31,261.00 | U.S. |
| 8 | McDonald's | 31,049.00 | U.S. |
| 9 | Disney | 29,251.00 | U.S. |
| 10 | Google | 25,590.00 | U.S. |
| 11 | Mercedes-Benz | 25,577.00 | Germany |
| 12 | Hewlett-Packard | 23,509.00 | U.S. |
| 13 | BMW | 23,298.00 | Germany |
| 14 | Gillette | 22,069.00 | U.S. |
| 15 | American Express | 21,940.00 | U.S. |
| 16 | Louis Vuitton | 21,602.00 | France |
| 17 | Cisco | 21,306.00 | U.S. |
| 18 | Marlboro | 21,300.00 | U.S. |
| 19 | Citi | 20,174.00 | U.S. |
| 20 | Honda | 19,079.00 | Japan |
| 21 | Samsung | 17,689.00 | S. Korea |
| 22 | H&M | 13,840.00 | Sweden |
| 23 | Oracle | 13,831.00 | U.S. |
| 24 | Apple | 13,724.00 | U.S. |
| 25 | Sony | 13,583.00 | Japan |
| 26 | Pepsi | 13,249.00 | U.S. |
| 27 | HSBC | 13,143.00 | Britain |
| 28 | Nescafe | 13,055.00 | Switzerland |
| 29 | Nike | 12,672.00 | U.S. |
| 30 | UPS | 12,621.00 | U.S. |
| 31 | SAP | 12,228.00 | Germany |
| 32 | Dell | 11,695.00 | U.S. |

| 2008 Rank | Brand | 2008 Brand Value ($ Millions) | Country of Ownership |
|---|---|---|---|
| 33 | Budweiser | 11,438.00 | U.S. |
| 34 | Merrill Lynch | 11,399.00 | U.S. |
| 35 | Ikea | 10,913.00 | Sweden |
| 36 | Canon | 10,876.00 | Japan |
| 37 | J.P. Morgan | 10,773.00 | U.S. |
| 38 | Goldman Sachs | 10,331.00 | U.S. |
| 39 | Kellogg's | 9,710.00 | U.S. |
| 40 | Nintendo | 8,772.00 | Japan |
| 41 | UBS | 8,740.00 | Switzerland |
| 42 | Morgan Stanley | 8,696.00 | U.S. |
| 43 | Philips | 8,325.00 | Netherlands |
| 44 | Thomson Reuters | 8,313.00 | Canada |
| 45 | Gucci | 8,254.00 | Italy |
| 46 | eBay | 7,991.00 | U.S. |
| 47 | Accenture | 7,948.00 | U.S. |
| 48 | Siemens | 7,943.00 | Germany |
| 49 | Ford | 7,896.00 | U.S. |
| 50 | Harley-Davidson | 7,609.00 | U.S. |
| 51 | L'Oreal | 7,508.00 | France |
| 52 | MTV | 7,193.00 | U.S. |
| 53 | Volkswagen | 7,047.00 | Germany |
| 54 | AIG | 7,022.00 | U.S. |
| 55 | AXA | 7,001.00 | France |
| 56 | Heinz | 6,646.00 | U.S. |
| 57 | Colgate | 6,437.00 | U.S. |
| 58 | Amazon.com | 6,434.00 | U.S. |
| 59 | Xerox | 6,393.00 | U.S. |
| 60 | Chanel | 6,355.00 | France |
| 61 | Wrigley's | 6,105.00 | U.S. |
| 62 | Zara | 5,955.00 | Spain |
| 63 | Nestlé | 5,592.00 | Switzerland |
| 64 | KFC | 5,582.00 | U.S. |
| 65 | Yahoo! | 5,496.00 | U.S. |
| 66 | Danone | 5,408.00 | France |
| 67 | Audi | 5,407.00 | Germany |
| 68 | Caterpillar | 5,288.00 | U.S. |

| 2008 Rank | Brand | 2008 Brand Value ($ Millions) | Country of Ownership |
| --- | --- | --- | --- |
| 69 | Avon | 5,264.00 | U.S. |
| 70 | Adidas | 5,072.00 | Germany |
| 71 | Rolex | 4,956.00 | Switzerland |
| 72 | Hyundai | 4,846.00 | S. Korea |
| 73 | BlackBerry | 4,802.00 | Canada |
| 74 | Kleenex | 4,636.00 | U.S. |
| 75 | Porsche | 4,603.00 | Germany |
| 76 | Hermès | 4,575.00 | France |
| 77 | Gap | 4,357.00 | U.S. |
| 78 | Panasonic | 4,281.00 | Japan |
| 79 | Cartier | 4,236.00 | France |
| 80 | Tiffany & Co | 4,208.00 | U.S. |
| 81 | Pizza Hut | 4,097.00 | U.S. |
| 82 | Allianz | 4,033.00 | Germany |
| 83 | Moet & Chandon | 3,951.00 | France |
| 84 | BP | 3,911.00 | Britain |
| 85 | Starbucks | 3,879.00 | U.S. |
| 86 | ING | 3,768.00 | Netherlands |
| 87 | Motorola | 3,721.00 | U.S. |
| 88 | Duracell | 3,682.00 | U.S. |
| 89 | Smirnoff | 3,590.00 | Britain |
| 90 | Lexus | 3,588.00 | Japan |
| 91 | Prada | 3,585.00 | Italy |
| 92 | Johnson & Johnson | 3,582.00 | U.S. |
| 93 | Ferrari | 3,527.00 | Italy |
| 94 | Armani | 3,526.00 | Italy |
| 95 | Hennessy | 3,513.00 | France |
| 96 | Marriott | 3,502.00 | U.S. |
| 97 | Shell | 3,471.00 | Netherlands |
| 98 | Nivea | 3,401.00 | Germany |
| 99 | FedEx | 3,359.00 | U.S. |
| 100 | Visa | 3,338.00 | U.S. |
| | Total | 1,213,774.00 | |

Source: *Businessweek*

## What's Left After Integrity Is Abused?

INTEGRITY CAN GO to waste if, at the leadership level, strategy and guidance go astray. That's essentially what happened during the 2008 financial crisis. The bosses of some big banks took unreasonable risks and ultimately drove their companies to the brink of collapse. The bank was like a fine car with first-class design and engineering. But it doesn't matter how great the car is if the person at the wheel drives recklessly and ends up going off the road.

In the panic of 2008, critical problems occurred at the driver level. The heads of the banks directed or permitted their institutions to take imprudent risks. They focused on trying to make money quickly without providing long-term value to their customers. It's interesting to think what might have happened if the banks had implemented Toyota's system of pull cords to alert everyone to quality problems. Things might have turned out differently. High quality, after all, is about giving customers what they have been promised. It's hard to imagine that the banks truly believed the risky mortgage-related products they were selling delivered lasting value to their clients.

Still, it's important to remember that while the financial system was badly damaged by the panic, it was not destroyed. The great fear as everything started to unravel in 2008 was that the whole system would collapse. That didn't happen. There's still a lot of built-up integrity that keeps financial activity going.

Putting the damage in context, the basic mechanisms of the system never changed. They are still extremely valuable. Even after credit markets seized up in the fall of 2008, trading in many assets continued. Trading volumes can fall as economic activity declines, but market participants of all kinds continue to trade. Investment banks, commercial banks, investment companies, and government entities can still rely on their trading operations as they did before the panic. On any given day, billions of dollars are still traded in the bond market despite the turmoil of 2008. The same held for other markets like stocks, commodities, and foreign exchange.

It's clear that the public didn't abandon investing in stocks, bonds, and other financial instruments. And despite sharp losses reported by mutual funds in 2008, small investors did not turn away from mutual fund investments either. There's a lot of trust remaining in the industry. As of November 2008, mutual funds still held $9.3 trillion worth of financial assets.

The point to remember is that despite the worst panic since the Great Depression, the U.S. financial system continued to function. That's because a durable and valuable arrangement of financial machinery underlies the system. That machinery has generated economic wealth and prosperity for the nation for decades.

Still, the panic of 2008 showed that the financial system can and should be both improved and operated more effectively. By understanding the critical role integrity plays, we can devise ways of creating more of it and thereby increase our economic well-being. Investing in integrity is a way forward to create a better, stronger financial system. It offers tremendous opportunities for the rest of the economy too. Creating integrity is not wishful thinking. It's a practical and strategic approach to building a healthier economy.

## CHAPTER EIGHT

# Lessons from a Start-Up

. . . . . . . . . . . . . . . . . . . . . . . . . . . .

Think back to a time when the economy was booming and the Internet first captured our imagination. A small start-up specializing in online auctions planned to go public. The initial reaction from investors was cautious. Many wondered how the company could grow when its business depended on complete strangers trusting each other. Why would buyers and sellers follow through in an Internet auction? A buyer could make a winning bid and then simply walk away. And a seller could take the cash and abscond. Skeptics thought that while the Web site might manage to attract a small following, it was unlikely to go anywhere.

Typical of the era, the company had a funny name: eBay.

By the time of its IPO in September 1998, senior executives had convinced enough investors to back the firm and the offering was a huge success. On the first day of trading, the fledgling company was valued at $2 billion. Better yet, its business expanded rapidly. By the end of 2008, it was generating $8 billion in revenues. Most incredibly, though, 88 million strangers had trusted each other enough to buy and sell on eBay again and again.

No one imagined how successful eBay would be. Even the founders of the company were taken aback by the extent of its popularity and explosive growth. Not only did a business based on trust actually work, it worked extremely well. Was eBay just plain lucky or was there something else involved?

In the beginning, growth was driven by a virtuous cycle. First, a small group of buyers and sellers came together in a relationship of trust that benefited both sides and led to an economic payoff for everyone involved—buyers, sellers, and eBay. Word spread quickly over the Internet of the trustworthiness of the site. More sellers and buyers tried eBay, driving more growth and more wealth. The more users came to the site, the more it drew in others who needed or wanted a big market to trade in. The eBay site had created an integrity system, a system where buyers and sellers treated each other fairly and unlocked economic benefits that were previously unavailable.

It was a remarkable accomplishment. From scratch, eBay had built a platform where users had an incentive to behave honorably and where their integrity and trust were rewarded. Not only did eBay make shareholders better off, it made a whole community better off. By connecting people who wanted to trade and otherwise had little opportunity to do so, eBay created a useful service that hadn't previously existed.

The eBay site did not eliminate cheating, though. There were still cases of fraud, cheating, and bad behavior. And as the company grew, the number of problems related to abuses and fraud also increased. In 2008 the company seemed to hit a ceiling, as the number of users leveled off, and management came under pressure to find new sources of revenue. Once a darling of investors, eBay fell out of favor.

The lesson of eBay, though, is not to hold it up as a perfect business model. Nor should we naively assume that it could keep growing forever. The critical point to learn from eBay is how it got millions of complete strangers to trust each other in the first place.

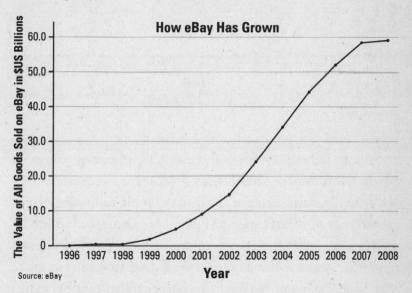

Source: eBay

## How eBay Was Born

IT ALL STARTED with Pierre Omidyar, the founder of eBay. Omidyar was twenty-eight and living in San Jose, California, when he first wrote the code that became the basis for the on-line auction site. It was the mid-1990s.

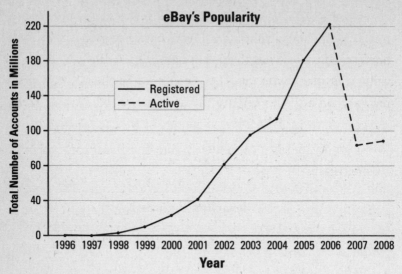

In 2007, eBay switched from tracking registered users to active users.
Source: eBay

While writing software for a small technology company by day, Omidyar, a French-born Iranian, was experimenting with the Internet at night. Fascinated with technology from an early age, Omidyar was intrigued when someone bid $14.93 on a broken laser pointer he had posted for sale. Thinking the buyer had made a mistake, Omidyar contacted him to make sure he knew it was broken. The buyer replied that he was in fact a collector of broken laser pointers. It was the first inkling Omidyar had that he was on to something.

Starting with a mix of computer, collectible, and quirky items like dolls and toys, traffic on the site quickly grew. In a matter of months, Omidyar found he was actually taking in more money than he was spending to run the site, and he turned his full attention to it.

As he worked on the Web site, Omidyar kept one thing in mind. He believed that people were basically good and should be allowed to do what they were naturally inclined to do. It's a value that many who joined the company in the beginning say really stood out. Jim Griffith, eBay's dean of education, joined the company in 1996, when users totaled in the thousands, not millions. He recalls being deeply skeptical about Omidyar's worldview. "I never believed people were basically good," he said. "It took an exposure to Pierre's ethos and meeting buyers and sellers over and over again to understand. I could count on one hand the number of people who are generally bad. This is out of millions of people. It's changed the way I view the world."

In the very beginning, when only a few auctions were held a day, Omidyar would tell buyers and sellers how to behave. "Deal with others the way you would have them deal with you," he wrote in a letter on the site in 1996. "Remember you are usually dealing with individuals, just like yourself. Subject to making mistakes. Well-meaning but wrong on occasion. That's just human."

Omidyar believed that buyers and sellers should work out differences among themselves. He didn't have the time or inclination to get involved. He saw eBay simply as a venue—a place where people came together online to trade. His approach to the marketplace was very hands off.

In the early days, Omidyar wasn't thinking about imposing rules or setting up procedures for dealing with complaints, but as the company grew, he and others at the firm found it necessary to adjust that view. Over time, eBay users wanted the company itself to get more involved. Buyers and sellers wanted eBay to intervene in disputes, set some ground rules, and provide a bit more structure.

Jim Griffith describes the early days on eBay as like being in a small town. Everyone knew one another and knew that the consequences of doing something bad would be serious. You might be ostracized or even kicked out entirely.

But as the town grew, it became harder for users to know one another and there was a greater need to police the site. The company responded by introducing a few key changes, which served as the platform for increased integrity and trust in the growth years. In the process, eBay's role changed. No longer did it simply provide the venue. It was providing a basic framework, moderating disputes, and enforcing rules.

## Feedback

THE BACKBONE OF eBay was a feedback system. Introduced early on, it underwent several modifications, but the basic principle remained the same. Users of eBay get feedback on how they conduct themselves from other users. This was critical for two reasons.

First, the feedback system provided users with an incentive to behave well. If a seller didn't behave well, say by shipping a product that was in poorer shape than described, the buyer could report the discrepancy and it would show on the seller's record. At the same time, if a user delivered as promised, positive feedback could be reported and recorded too.

All that feedback was taken by eBay and tallied in what amounted to a score-keeping system. Feedback scores were added up and indicated by how many stars a seller had next to his or her name. The highest feedback scores, over 10,000, were awarded a shooting star. And the highest of those was a red shooting star, for over 100,000 feedback points. The star rating system became a point of pride among sellers, and they quickly learned to protect their online reputations.

Second, the feedback system effectively brought everything out into the open. Users couldn't hide bad behavior, and good behavior was rewarded. By looking back at the ratings, users could see who they were transacting with and decide whether to proceed.

Initially, eBay's feedback system wasn't tied to a transaction. Omidyar believed that users should give both good and bad feedback about any interaction they had with fellow users. Sellers who readily answered each other's questions could be praised. Others who behaved rudely were exposed. In a sense, it was more about how people conducted themselves as members of the eBay community than about the trade itself.

But as the number of users grew, the company discovered that some users were manipulating feedback for their own purposes. They were getting others to leave good feedback to boost their scores when it wasn't warranted and sending bad feedback to hurt someone else's reputation.

After four years, eBay decided it needed to adjust the feedback mechanism. Instead of being about any interaction with a user, feedback scores were tied to transactions. That way, only people participating legitimately in the auction process could offer feedback about a buyer or seller.

In 2008, eBay changed the feedback system again. After talking with a number of major buyers who expressed dissatisfaction with the site, the company discovered a high incidence of retaliation feedback.

It worked like this: A buyer unhappy with a particular seller left negative feedback about that seller. The seller, not wanting bad feedback scores, retaliated and left negative feedback about the buyer. Then the seller asked the buyer to drop the whole thing, and both sides agreed to withdraw their negative feedback. The buyer who was unjustly accused of bad behavior might agree, but it wasn't a positive experience. In effect, bad behavior could be swept under the rug and be repeated.

To address this problem, eBay decided to stop sellers from giving feedback to buyers. Buyers could continue to leave feedback about sellers, as that information flow was critical to buyer confidence. But if a buyer behaved badly, the seller would have to open a dispute, which eBay would oversee and mediate.

The eBay feedback system has evolved, but it remains an important way of establishing trust between buyers and sellers who don't know each other and may only engage in a single transaction. And the proof lies in the fact that some of eBay's competitors have tried to copy it.

When Amazon.com first began selling online in 1995, it included customer reviews of books. There was nothing to prevent authors from posting rave reviews of their work. Today, though, Amazon asks customers to rate reviews as helpful or not helpful. The helpful reviews then move to the top of the list and the unhelpful ones to the bottom, allowing customers to sort through what they are reading. Customer feedback about reviews has been valuable in a number of ways. It encourages people who write reviews to think about doing their best, not just dashing something off without thinking. And with more confidence in the quality of reviews, Amazon can attract more customers to its site.

## The Bulletin Board

THE FEEDBACK SYSTEM wasn't the only thing eBay came up with. Another critical step was to introduce an electronic bulletin board.

Omidyar set up the bulletin board on the site as a way for eBay users to talk to each other and answer each other's questions. Over time, it became a critical way for eBay management to communicate with customers, understand their needs, and quickly implement changes.

As far as Omidyar was concerned, eBay users were not just customers but members of a community. It was an important distinction. By treating eBay users as members of a community, eBay instilled a sense of responsibility into those using the site.

In the early days, regular eBay users acted just like a small community. Discussion wasn't limited to the site. Friendships blossomed, and there was a sense of ownership in discussions of how to look after the community and behave. Interesting and quirky personalities became larger-than-life characters and generated a sense of interest and belonging. Importantly, this fostered a sense among users of wanting the site to succeed. It also proved a valuable way for eBay management to find out exactly what its customers needed.

Frequently, Omidyar would tell his fledgling staff to be patient with users and, most importantly, to be responsive. It worked. Early users of the site tended to be loyal to eBay, and those numbers of loyal users formed a critical mass that attracted others away from competing online auction sites that were springing up at the time.

The management of eBay was responsible for the site but also gave users a sense of having a stake in what was happening. It was a powerful incentive to act appropriately while present on the site.

The bulletin board served eBay as an information source. When eBay decided to prohibit the sale of firearms on its site in February 1999, it simply announced that the change had been made. There was a huge outcry and a backlash against the site. Management learned from that time to communicate more openly with users and give them warning about proposed changes far in advance. Six months later, they faced far less resistance when they explained to the community ahead of time that they had to limit the sale of certain alcohol and tobacco products.

## Simple Rules

TOGETHER, THE FEEDBACK ratings and the bulletin board were critical to the growth of eBay. But there was another factor too: making sure that the rules for buying or selling on the site were clear, straightforward, and intuitive.

Every aspect of doing business on the site was detailed in a straightforward manner that was easy to read and understand. Things like understanding user agreements, how to leave feedback, and how to report inappropriate behavior were all explained. The Web site detailed the kind of behavior that eBay considered inappropriate and the types of complaints it would and would not investigate. Once users read the rules, they had little doubt about what was expected of them when using the site.

For buyers, the rules were straightforward. The single most important thing a buyer had to do was to follow through on a bid. It was not okay to make a bid on eBay, have that bid accepted, and then walk away from the deal. When a buyer won the auction, the sale had to go through.

For sellers, the rules were similarly intuitive. Sellers must honestly describe the product they were selling and the condition it was in, and they must deliver what they said they would deliver in the agreed timeframe.

The rules for buyers and sellers were effective because they amounted to both parties doing what they would expect if the roles were reversed. They intuitively understood what to do and weren't asked to do anything complicated or unnatural. As a result, it was easy for people to follow the rules.

A few rules were quirky and a bit more difficult to understand. For instance, there was a rule that stopped sellers from saying their product was "like new." The reason was to help buyers looking for new items—for example, shoes—to avoid sorting through pages of used shoes they didn't want. Sellers frequently broke this rule since it wasn't intuitively understood.

The rules on eBay have been adjusted to take into account the experience of users over time. When a new situation arises, eBay addresses it. Even though its changes haven't always been universally popular, the fact that users can see eBay working on their behalf is an important element of their trust.

## Enforcing the Rules

IN CREATING THEIR platform of trust, eBay has learned how to act as an enforcer. There were some auctions that resulted in users being kicked off the site. Typically these were cases of fraud or interfering with the Web site. But at times, eBay has had to shut down auctions that were inappropriate or potentially illegal. When one person tried to sell a kidney to the highest bidder in September 1999, eBay shut down the auction.

For the most part, eBay found that problems on its site arose from misunderstandings rather than outright cheating. Relationships can be tricky at the best of times, but over the Internet, where there's no way to look a person in the eye or hear a voice at the end of the phone, matters can be made worse. All a buyer or seller has to go on is the written word, which sometimes can have more than one meaning.

According to eBay, the number of cases of fraud increased in line with growth in the number of registered users. That means that while the number of cases has increased, the rate of fraud hasn't changed. As reported by eBay, the rate of fraud is very low, perhaps as little as 0.01 percent. Of course, that figure may be too low, as some fraud may go unreported and undetected.

When it came to addressing destructive behavior, eBay learned to be vigilant. It found that a small number of bad sellers could quickly drive buyers off the site. If a buyer had a bad experience, it wasn't hard to tell thousands of total strangers via the Internet. Trying to give users a good experience on the site was a big focus of management in the early years. And it remains a key factor that will determine the company's future success.

## Putting It All Together: Creating an Integrity System

FROM THE OUTSET, Omidyar designed a system that allowed users a degree of freedom. His own belief was that it was in people's best interest to behave with integrity, and he created a system that rewarded good behavior. He never tried to stamp out cheating on the site. It never occurred to him to do that. Omidyar understood that by trading honestly, people would have more opportunity to trade in the future, and that meant they could do more business and create more wealth.

Several key factors fostered the relationship of trust between buyers and sellers on eBay. The most important was the feedback system, which brought behavior out into the open for all to see. Rating the way a seller behaved not only gave sellers the incentive to behave well, but it allowed buyers to have a level of confidence in the person they were dealing with.

Importantly, the feedback system also provided users with a platform for building long-term relationships. Sellers know their feedback scores are important in building their reputation and trustworthiness. Every sale happens in the context of a longer-term relationship, not a one-off with people that don't matter. Buyers who have a good experience tend to come back and attract other buyers.

Knowing what happens in a dispute has been important to building trust in the eBay marketplace too. Having the confidence that eBay is actively policing the site and making judgments about what is and isn't ethical instills a sense of trust among users and community.

Trust between buyers and sellers has been critical, but so too has trust between users and the company itself. Opening up lines of communication, responding to customers, and quickly addressing problems on the site were critical to eBay's initial success and the financial success of its shareholders and employees. Like Toyota, Omidyar was primarily concerned with building a site that worked for users, where they could trade and come away with important benefits. In other words, he focused on delivering lasting value. And it resulted in a big financial payoff for everyone: eBay's employees, shareholders, and users.

## Other Integrity Systems

AMONG MANY OTHER examples of integrity systems, perhaps the greatest of all is the New York Stock Exchange. Dating back to 1792, the stock exchange was designed as a place to make money. The idea was to establish a central location where people could meet and buy or sell stocks.

But it wasn't sufficient simply to provide a meeting place. Over time, the NYSE set rules and requirements for members and traders, instituted mechanisms for settlement and disclosure, and enforced its rules. When the NYSE first started, it had twenty-four members. Today there are thousands. The number of shares traded daily has exploded over the years. In 1886, 1 million shares traded daily. By 2007, 5 billion shares was the norm.

Another example of an integrity system is the Grameen Bank. Started in Bangladesh in the 1970s, the Grameen Bank has been replicated around the world as an effective way to lend to the poor and create wealth in the process.

In this system, borrowers join together as a group to access small sums of money, primarily for cottage industries. They are not required to have any collateral or sign any legal documents. Each group of borrowers has five members and they are expected to look after each other and make sure nobody defaults. The bank and the members of the group meet regularly to make sure no individual falls into repayment difficulties. The system is based on long-term relationships of trust between the borrower, the banker, and the other members of the community.

Over time, the bank has grown steadily. By the end of 2008, the Grameen Bank in Bangladesh had 7.61 million borrowers, 97 percent of them women. Since it began, the bank has lent out a total of more than $7 billion and has a repayment rate of 98 percent. Its fund are credited with helping the very poor in Bangladesh educate their children, and the founder, Muhammad Yunus, won the Noble Peace Prize in 2006 for his work.

## The Characteristics of Integrity Systems

As DIVERSE AS they are, eBay, the NYSE, and the Grameen Bank share certain characteristics.

Each involves a systematic effort to share facts openly. Bringing the truth out in the open is a crucial factor in any system of integrity. When behavior is hidden, the temptation to deal dishonestly is too great to resist. At eBay, rating a seller's past behavior means that everyone can see how honestly that seller behaves. And in the case of the Grameen Bank, regular meetings between the banker and community members ensure the flow of information. At those meetings, the lender can see how the individual is doing, whether the work is going well or not, and whether any unexpected circumstances have come up. Importantly, the bank encourages relationships with borrowers that are honest and open.

Second, each involves a carefully developed set of rules. In every instance the rules have been updated and refined over time to increase productivity and efficiency. Significant efforts ensure that the rules are clear, well understood, and easy to follow. Old, obsolete, or inefficient regulations are regularly replaced by newer and more efficient ones. The common good of participants in the marketplace, both buyers and sellers, is the touchstone for creating a better and more valuable marketplace.

At eBay, the rules governing buyer and seller reinforce the way a typical buyer or seller would want to be treated. Simplicity is critical. At the Grameen Bank, if borrowers with little formal education were saddled with overly bureaucratic rules, participation would suffer. Instead, the main rule is simple: repay the loan. Nothing else compares in importance.

Third, people operating in each system have considerable confidence that cheating the system won't pay. They know that cheaters will be caught and corrective action will be taken. When it changed its feedback rules to prevent retaliatory feedback, eBay understood that buyers needed to have confidence that the system was sound. And at the NYSE, members and traders are well aware that if they break the rules they are likely to get caught and could be expelled.

An integrity-creating system has all three of these components: thorough disclosure, clear and well-founded rules, and an effective system for dealing with violators. Those characteristics create the right conditions to promote integrity. And the more integrity, the more wealth, leading to a virtuous circle. Throughout the economy, simple and elegant integrity mechanisms create wealth.

But when we fail to take integrity into account, we can go considerably astray. Had eBay's Omidyar or the Grameen Bank's Yunus been deeply suspicious of people, it is doubtful that eBay or the Grameen Bank would still be around and operating successfully. On the one hand, they could have put in place overly restrictive rules, or added costly bonding and insurance requirements. On the other, they could have allowed a free-for-all that might have been hijacked by a few bad apples. But instead they struck a brilliant balance, creating a basic system or framework that, rather than being restrictive, actually sets participants free to achieve goals they couldn't achieve without it.

The modern political approach to integrity can at times fail miserably. It's too often about a show of toughness, making everybody jump through hoops and threatening violators with heavy penalties. The stated goal is often to eliminate wrongdoing. That's not wrong in itself, but it misses the much larger point. Unless there is a conscious effort to create a self-reinforcing system, writing rules to show "toughness" about whatever caused the latest crisis tends both to put unwelcome burdens on the honest and herd the unethical into new, not yet prohibited misadventures.

The U.S. tax code is the poster child for missing the target. It's so grotesquely complicated that virtually no one can be sure of being in exact compliance and paying fairly on his or her income. On paper there are heavy penalties for cheating, but in practice enforcement is lax. Perhaps most important, it has bred resentment among virtually all of those that it should be benefiting. What ought to be shocking rates of noncompliance come as no surprise.

Instead, a mind-set that seeks to create lasting value will invest in integrity and yield a host of positive benefits for the economy. Well-designed systems that encourage people to act honestly do just that.

## CHAPTER NINE

# The DNA of Integrity

..............................

Integrity evolved over centuries, but progress wasn't always uniform. At times integrity seemed under attack or even in decline. Some scandals and dramatic frauds have caused the public to question its existence. The spectacular South Sea Bubble of 1720 is still remembered today. A stock market bubble formed when shares in the South Sea Company began a remarkable run-up from around a hundred to a thousand pounds on what turned out to be exaggerated claims about the value of its monopoly on the slave trade. The tremendous rise in the stock price encouraged a host of other companies to form, many of which turned out to be totally fraudulent. One sought funding for "a design which will hereafter be promulgated," another "for a wheel for perpetual motion." In reaction, the British Parliament passed a law restricting the formation of joint stock companies, the forerunners of the modern corporation. But in trying to prevent a repeat of the bubble, the government probably missed the mark. As we now know, the form of the company wasn't the problem—the fraud and dishonesty were. Yet it wasn't until 1825 that the so-called Bubble Act was repealed.

Today we have far better tools at hand. In the aftermath of a crisis, strategic thinking about integrity can lead to significant economic gains. Integrity is something we can learn to cultivate. Using the basic building blocks of integrity we can invest in our collective integrity assets and, as a result, our wealth. We can create integrity systems that are self-reinforcing and can grow by themselves. The starting place is the DNA of integrity.

At the nucleus of our integrity assets lie three basic ideas, the genetic code for a system of trust: disclosure, norms, and accountability. Replicated millions of times, honed to efficiency by natural market selection, these three concepts are the key to investing in integrity.

Disclosure, norms, and accountability are already widely utilized. But using them together with an economic objective, to efficiently create a self-reinforcing system producing repeated increases in integrity, is an exciting new prospect.

## The Open Market

IN THE RUN-UP to the great stock market crash of 1929, public companies were not required to release specific information to the investing public. If corporate management wanted to disclose facts, they could; if they didn't, that was their choice. The crash showed that too few investors understood what they were actually investing in. Out of the $50 billion worth of new securities issued prior to the crash, half became worth-less.

After 1934, public companies were required to release full, fair, and timely information to the public that was accessible and easy to use. That system of mandated disclosure became the centerpiece of the Securities and Exchange Commission and is a good example of disclosure that created value.

The basic principle that public companies must report fi-nancial and other relevant information to the public was a crit-ical factor behind the popularity and growth of the U.S. stock market. In the United States, the public has such confidence in the stock market that the nation's entire system of saving for retirement relies heavily on making investments in public companies. That wouldn't be the case without the mandated disclosure system that has become so ingrained in America's investing culture.

The simple idea behind the mandated disclosure system was to give investors a baseline of facts. Given that infor-mation, investors could decide for themselves whether they wanted to buy, sell, or hold individual stocks. It was a bril-liantly conceived idea, and a simple and elegant policy. In the aftermath of the worst stock market crash ever and during a time of major integrity breaches, policy makers didn't try to limit the way companies behaved to prevent another crash. And they weren't trying to impose hundreds of rules to catch companies out if they committed fraud. Instead, in a single stroke, they designed a system that allowed companies to operate as they saw fit as long as they were open about what they were doing. That way, the public could decide whether it would hand over investment dollars. It was a critical factor in restoring America's badly shaken trust in the stock market following the great crash.

Of course, the SEC's disclosure system isn't perfect. Over time, the reporting requirements for public companies have become more complicated and onerous. Yet the mandated disclosure system is still widely seen as helping to allocate capital efficiently in the economy. When information flows, markets work. If anything, in the aftermath of the 2008 panic, pressure has been building to extend the mandated disclosure system to other areas of financial markets in order to restore confidence and increase efficiency.

The point of disclosure is to bring the truth out into the open and allow people to make their own decisions. That inspires trust in the system, promotes efficiency, and creates value.

## The "Rules of the Road"

EACH DAY MILLIONS of Americans get into cars and drive according to the traffic laws. There's little doubt in drivers' minds about what is expected. Everyone knows to drive on the right-hand side of the road, stop at red lights, and so on. And most important, we all understand why.

Americans understand that it makes sense to have a system of rules to get people to their destinations efficiently and safely. Anyone who has driven in other parts of the world where traffic rules are less well defined can immediately appreciate the benefits of clear road rules. Not only can it be frighten-

ing and downright dangerous, but road chaos is far less efficient.

. . . . . . . . . . . . . . . . . . . . . . . . . . . . . . . . . . . . . . . . . . . .

## Global Incidence of Traffic Deaths

Over 90 percent of the world's fatalities on the roads occur in low-income and middle-income
countries, which have only 48 percent of the world's registered vehicles.

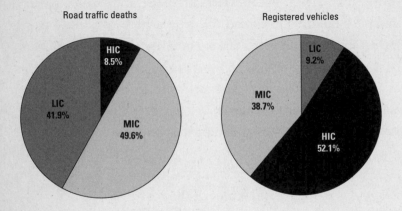

*Road Traffic Deaths and Registered Motorized Vehicles, by Income Group*

Road traffic fatality rates in low-income and middle-income countries (21.5 and 19.5 per
100,000 population, respectively) are double the rates in high-income countries (10.3 per 100,000).

Source: Global status report on road safety. Geneva, World Health Organization, 2009

Disclosure is essential in promoting integrity, but it isn't
enough. Clear and simple standards that are universally understood are critical. The clear standards of traffic laws establishing the "rules of the road" are an example. So why do the rules
of the road work?

For the most part they are clear, consistent, and make intuitive sense. The basic rules of right-hand driving, red lights,

and stop signs have been largely unchanged since they were first introduced. Those rules are learned at an early age and internalized. From childhood, we're conditioned to stop automatically when we see a red light.

Even more important, the system is self-reinforcing. Drivers let each other know when they're doing something wrong, by either honking or flashing their headlights and occasionally even by vivid expression. Anyone who has accidentally turned the wrong way down a one-way street knows that a sharp blast from nearby can quickly correct the error. It's the ability to see other drivers on the road and provide feedback that promotes compliance with traffic laws. Parking is another instance. In an unfamiliar neighborhood, checking how other cars are parked helps a driver follow parking rules. Integrity systems can be incredibly powerful when they are self-reinforcing.

Clear and simple rules are essential in any system, but so is a thoughtful approach to the rules themselves. It's a fine balance between giving people enough room to operate and providing boundaries in which to do that. Well-made rules are not restrictive; they are enabling. The secret of eBay was to achieve that balance. Its founder didn't set out thinking about rules for an online auction Web site. Over time, he established a simple framework so that users understood how they should behave. Setting up standards or rules with the clear intention of promoting integrity is about setting people free to do the right thing.

Investing in integrity provides a way out of the regulation versus free market quagmire. In recent decades, the conventional way of thinking has been that rules restrict activity and are therefore bad. That led to a false choice between a market system without rules and rules that only restrict activity.

That thinking leads to a dead end. No market exists without rules. The rules of the game are an essential part of any system that hopes to operate efficiently. Take the New York Stock Exchange. The NYSE has plenty of rules (probably too many!) about what members can and can't do. Yet those rules actually help the system operate and create wealth for members as well as for the society at large.

When thinking about integrity in an economic sense, an essential goal to keep in mind is that rules should be simple. Clarity brings efficiency and enables the system to be self-reinforcing. In order words, smart, effective rules will leave plenty of room for innovation and entrepreneurial risk taking but require appropriate disclosure and inhibit efforts to exploit the trust of others. Well made, rules can promote a culture of integrity in which people internalize wealth-producing principles.

## Calculating Getting Caught

FOR THE MOST part, we drive according to the local traffic rules automatically. Yet there are a few notable exceptions. In the United States, speed limits couldn't be clearer or simpler, yet they are seldom obeyed. Why do so many people ignore these laws?

Drivers speed when they don't expect to get caught.

Behind the wheel of a well-engineered car on a wide open freeway, the impulse to speed can be great. Who's going to care, after all? Or how about a crowded road when everyone is traveling above the speed limit? Safety in numbers may be the rationale in that case. But in either situation, speeding depends on a perception about the probability of being caught. Unless that probability increases substantially, speeding is likely to remain prevalent.

Increased enforcement can change behavior. Almost a million and a half Americans were arrested for drunk driving in 2007. The number of Americans who drive with blood alcohol levels above the legal limit without being caught is believed to be significantly higher. Yet the rules in each state about blood alcohol limits are quite strict.

Here too the problem is that drivers who drink and drive believe there is a very good chance they won't get caught. As long as they obey the traffic rules and drive within the speed limit, there's no reason for the police to suspect they've been drinking. If they get pulled over, then a police officer is likely to check their blood alcohol level.

It's a problem of accountability that other countries have found solutions to. Australia uses random breath testing, which is widely considered to be responsible for reducing the number of people who drive above the legal blood alcohol limit. According to the World Health Organization, over a thirty-year period to 2001, alcohol as a factor in car crashes in Australia almost halved. In cities like Melbourne and Sydney, "booze buses," as random breath-testing units are commonly called, have become part of the daily landscape. The WHO has found

# Blood Alcohol Limits Around the World

*Blood Alcohol Concentration Limits (g/dl) by Country/Area*

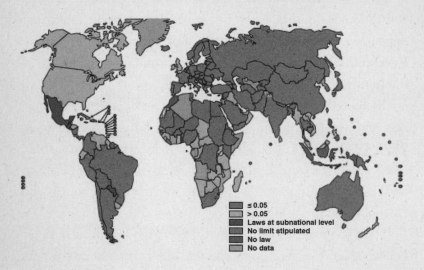

≤ 0.05
\> 0.05
Laws at subnational level
No limit stipulated
No law
No data

## Drunk Driving

The World Health Organization (WHO) has found that drinking and driving increases both the risk of a crash and the likelihood that death or a serious injury will result. The risk of involvement in a crash increases significantly above blood alcohol concentration (BAC) levels of 0.04 gram per decilitre (g/dl). A blood alcohol concentration limit of less than or equal to 0.05 g/dl is recommended for the general population.

A survey by the WHO found that less than half of countries worldwide have drunk-driving laws based on a blood alcohol concentration limit that is equal to or less than 0.05 grams per decilitre.

Source: Global status report on road safety. Geneva, World Health Organization, 2009

that in most countries the level of enforcement of drunk-driving laws has a direct effect on the incidence of drinking and driving. Increasing drivers' perception of the risk of being caught is an effective means of preventing drunk driving.

While enforcing speed limits and drunk-driving laws tends to be patchy in the United States, a high degree of energy and thoroughness go into enforcing homicide laws. Think about it for a moment. Most people probably don't expect to get away with murder. It's understood that if a murder is committed, there's a fairly good chance the person who committed the crime will be caught. And that perception is backed up by the facts. Compared with all major violent crimes, murder has the highest arrest rate.

In 2007, the FBI reported that the number of cases of murder and nonnegligent manslaughter in the United States was 16,929. In the same period, 13,480 arrests were made. That suggests an arrest rate of 80 percent.

And the penalty for murder is high. Long sentences are routine, and some states still have the death penalty. The combination of a high likelihood of getting caught with a big penalty puts murder off-limits for the vast majority of people.

From an economic perspective, the point of accountability is not to punish people. It's to give the public the expectation that if they break the rules there will be consequences. In other words, the threat of enforcement has to be real enough that it seems more likely they will get caught than not. And if they get caught, the penalty has to be large enough to help discourage the behavior. Ideally, under these conditions, people's behavior will change and punishment will rarely be necessary.

It's easy to set up systems where penalties are high but there's little chance of getting caught. But it's hard to imagine a company like Toyota getting quality by occasionally catching a mistake and firing a worker.

· · · · · · · · · · · · · · · · · · · · · · · · · · · · · · · · · · · · · · · · · · · · · · · · · ·

## The Likelihood of Getting Caught

| Crime | Number of Cases in 2007 | Number of Arrests in 2007 | Estimated Arrest Rate (%) |
|---|---|---|---|
| Murder and nonnegligent manslaughter | 16,929 | 13,480 | 80 |
| Forcible rape | 90,427 | 23,307 | 26 |
| Robbery | 445,125 | 126,715 | 28 |
| Burglary | 2,179,140 | 303,853 | 14 |
| Property crime | 9,843,481 | 1,610,088 | 16 |
| Larceny-theft | 6,568,572 | 1,172,762 | 18 |
| Motor vehicle theft | 1,095,769 | 118,231 | 11 |

Source: FBI's Uniform Crime Reporting Program, 2007 nationwide figures

· · · · · · · · · · · · · · · · · · · · · · · · · · · · · · · · · · · · · · · · · · · · · · · · · ·

## What Happens When the DNA of Integrity Is Missing?

IT'S A LITTLE-KNOWN fact that for a brief time during the Roaring Twenties, most tax returns were open to public inspection. It seems shocking by today's standards of privacy, but back then members of both parties believed it would promote accurate information that would benefit lawmakers and the public. "Secrecy is of the greatest aid to corruption," remarked one senator at the time.

Once the information was made public, all sorts of details emerged. For instance, the *New York Times* ran a story revealing that some prominent New Yorkers paid no taxes at all. After growing complaints financed by well-heeled opponents, the publicity requirement was dropped. Today, all corporate and individual tax returns remain private, the one exception being for presidential candidates. Since the 1970s it has been a tradition for presidential candidates to release their tax returns in what is widely seen as a test of their integrity. It's interesting to consider whether others ought to do the same. Social scientists guess that at least one in three Americans cheats the IRS.

Systems that intelligently combine disclosure, norms, and accountability have all the right ingredients to create integrity. It should come as no surprise that systems without these basic characteristics can be rife with cheating. The U.S. tax system is a prime example.

Not only have tax returns remained private, but over the years they have become secret too. In 1976, tax returns went from being considered public to being considered confidential records. Prior to 1976, the president could control access to tax returns. Individuals who could prove they had a material interest could be granted approval to access another person's tax returns. In addition, the IRS had lists of individuals who filed tax returns and could release that information. All that changed when the Nixon administration was accused of using tax information against opponents. As a result, the Tax Act of 1976 was passed, eliminating the ability of the president to disclose individual tax information. Stiff penalties were also put in place for anyone at the IRS or any state or federal government official who disclosed tax information to the public. That strict clampdown remains in effect today.

Keeping tax returns confidential seems so ingrained in our thinking that any proposal to open tax returns to the public would be met with skepticism. Even public companies, with all their disclosure requirements, don't have to come clean on what they report to the IRS. Most, in fact, keep two sets of books: one for the IRS and the other for everyone else. Just the idea of two sets of books seems disturbingly shady and secretive. That secrecy doesn't inspire trust. Hiding information usually only benefits the person doing the hiding. It seldom benefits the public.

In addition to a lack of disclosure, clear standards are missing from the tax code. Over time, the complexity of the code has grown to the point of absurdity. By 2008, it was more than thirteen thousand pages long. As the rules have become more complicated and filings longer, the number of Americans using some form of tax preparation service has jumped to more than 60 percent of all taxpayers. And the cost of all that complexity is high. The U.S. Treasury has estimated that cost at around $125 billion a year.

Not only are taxes incredibly laborious, they're often confusing as well. Government estimates put the cost of inaccuracies—intentional or inadvertent—as high as $350 billion a year.

The calculus many Americans appear to make is that cheating is worth taking the risk. After all, the chances of getting caught seem low. And they are indeed very low. In 2007, out of 134.5 million individual tax returns filed with the IRS, 1.38 million were subject to an audit. That is: 1 percent of all tax returns were audited. Out of that 1 percent, only 22 percent of the audits were conducted by agents or tax examiners; the remainder were handled by correspondence. While the odds do go up for returns reporting high income or for complex tax returns, on the whole, Americans know there's a good chance they won't be audited.

Without the benefits of disclosure, clear norms, and accountability, it's little wonder that millions of Americans cheat on their taxes. It's even become common for public officials to have trouble paying their taxes properly. In the first few weeks of President Obama's new administration, a string of officials appointed to senior positions were forced to come clean on their taxes. No less an individual than the secretary of the treasury, Timothy Geithner, apologized for making errors on his tax returns and paid back taxes.

A tax system in which the best advice for compliance is to hire an expert is unlikely to generate any goodwill to do the right thing. It's impossible to internalize all those rules. The self-reinforcing nature of integrity also works in reverse. When we think other people are cheating and getting away with it, we don't feel much like doing the right thing ourselves. That tends to encourage more cheating and puts a bigger drag on the economy.

But it doesn't have to be that way. The tax code could promote integrity. A tax system that was open, clear, and understandable, and made it likely that cheaters would get caught, would go a long way to changing our behavior. Recognizing that we can create a system that operates fairly and efficiently would be a step in the right direction.

Yet we need to think of it as a system. It's the combination of disclosure, norms, and accountability that promotes integrity. While each component is integrity enhancing, one or two components can't do the work of creating integrity alone. Making tax returns public won't by itself bring down rates of noncompliance when the system remains complex to the point of absurdity and is only haphazardly enforced.

Using the building blocks of integrity, we could move from our current system, whose unstated assumption is that you're crazy if you don't find ways to avoid paying taxes, to one that encourages people to pay taxes. If successful it could even become a system in which Americans feel a commitment to do the right thing and encourage others to do the same. Something like driving on the right-hand side of the road and staying in your lane.

One idea might be to disclose how much tax each individual pays in a given year. The information could be used in many interesting ways to enhance integrity. For instance, what if magazines like *Forbes* ran a list each year of the top one hundred taxpayers in the nation? Wouldn't that get the public's attention? Mightn't high-profile figures, concerned about their reputation and standing in the community, want to be on the list as a sign of their wealth and their integrity? In a single stroke it could be a powerful way to get top income earners to pay their taxes and inspire others to do the same.

## Designing Integrity Systems

GOING TO THE cupboard to find a bit of disclosure, norms, and accountability and throwing them together won't necessarily create integrity. They need to be combined in a thoughtful way that keeps in mind the ultimate goal: to create an integrity system that is simple, efficient, improves over time, and is self-reinforcing.

An integrity system should be designed to work naturally to reinforce itself. That means that people follow rules because it's in their self-interest. Some people may do the right thing just because it's ethical. But often people need encouragement. Part of encouraging good behavior is designing a system in which it makes sense to do the right thing.

Pierre Omidyar, eBay's founder, designed a system based on people's desire to trade objects and make money or gain satisfaction from a purchase. Omidyar understood that it was in the users' best interest to behave according to simple rules so that they could trade with each other. And he ensured that they saw the benefits of integrity. Once someone is kicked off eBay, there isn't a comparable auction site to join.

To design a self-reinforcing integrity system, two additional factors should be kept in mind: the power of long-term thinking and a mechanism that enables improvements—a feedback loop.

Integrity flourishes in long-term relationships. Over time there's a natural tendency to create integrity. That's because over the long run the truth ultimately comes out. It's much easier to hide the truth for a short while than it is to hide it over years and years. In the long run, people also learn and understand what is expected of them and they benefit from experience about what works well and what doesn't.

A relationship that survives over the long term, then, tends to have the DNA of integrity. Short-term relationships, on the other hand, are just the opposite. In fact, it's possible to view short-term thinking as a red flag for an integrity vacuum. There's little incentive to build a relationship of integrity and trust with a person you may never encounter again. That helps explain why it can be common among tourists to have bad experiences with locals when traveling. Local businesses looking to exploit the trust of others will tend to prey on people they don't expect to be back again.

The trick to creating integrity is to get people thinking about the long term. People acting as if they're in long-term relationships or doing things that are sustainable creates fertile ground for producing more integrity. That doesn't necessarily mean that every business relationship must be lasting. So long as people act as if they're in long-term relationships, they'll stay on track.

Recall that eBay was successful in this regard. The online auction site probably would never have worked if sellers had treated buyers with a short-term mentality. And in a sense they had every reason to. There's a good chance buyers won't return to the same seller after an auction is complete but move on to seek other products. Yet by implementing the feedback system, eBay effectively provided a mechanism by which buyers and sellers could act as if they were in a long-term relationship. A relationship with one buyer became a relationship with the entire buying community. Sellers understood that each transaction was part of a longer-term relationship with the community. As long as they wanted to sell on eBay, they had to act with integrity.

In the end, the aim of an integrity system is to foster a culture that doesn't look for short-term cheating opportunities but for long-term wealth-creating opportunities. How can it be achieved?

One place to look is redesigning compensation structures. What if we rewarded people for the work they did and the wealth they created over the long term rather than for their ability to make money in the short term? That way, they would have a vested interest in the health and well-being of the institution over the long term and wouldn't be looking for ways to extract as much money as they could in the short term regardless of what it did to others later on.

It turns out that part of the excessive risk taking in finance during the 2008 crisis was caused by compensation structures tied to rewards for short-term moneymaking. Bankers who could see an opportunity to make big money in the short term had enormous incentive to do so, regardless of the cost to the firm. Little of their remuneration was tied to how well the firm would do over the long term. So while selling risky products made money in the short term for a few, it effectively destroyed wealth in the long run for many others.

Tying compensation in part to the overall performance of the firm and not just a single division is a start, but setting it up over the long term is also necessary. Providing financial incentives for long-term wealth creation promotes a long-term relationship between the employee and the firm and can lead to other changes in thinking.

If people knew that their remuneration was tied to performance in the long term, wouldn't they be thinking of how to create products and services that were valuable over the long term? Wouldn't that help build long-term relationships with the customer too? That mentality might have big rewards not only for the customers and employees but for shareholders and the public at large. Toyota comes to mind here. Toyota has grown into the leading car company in the world not by trying to make as much money as it can in the short run but by satisfying car buyers over the long run.

Long-term thinking could transform other areas of the economy too. Wouldn't we think about the environment in an entirely different way if we took a long-term approach to generating wealth? Is extracting as much oil as we can and consuming it today really creating wealth? When we spew pollution into the air to manufacture goods, aren't we hindering our wealth-creating opportunities in the future?

Fiscal policy is another area we might consider differently. If we started to view the enormous accumulation of government debt and plans for greater indebtedness in a long-run wealth-creating context, we might judge our actions differently. Instead of promoting wealth, massive debt burdens could be judged to be hurting our ability to generate wealth in the future in much the same way as killing off the goose that lays the golden eggs.

The point to appreciate is that investing in integrity is all about sustainable wealth creation, a path forward that avoids the pitfalls of crises that can wreak havoc on the global economy.

Incorporating a feedback loop is also critical. At the outset, it's often hard to know what rules will end up working better than others. Think about eBay when it first started out. Omidyar had never built an online auction before. When he began, he had in mind a system that allowed buyers and sellers to work out their problems among themselves. It wasn't long before he realized that would never do. Buyers and sellers often couldn't solve disputes among themselves. They needed rules and a third party to mediate. As a result, he designed a basic framework for how to operate on eBay. Over time that framework has been adapted and improved as it became clear what worked and what didn't. The willingness of eBay to listen to feedback from its users and make changes based on that feedback has been an essential element of the site's success.

Or think of Toyota. Its ability to deliver what customers want has relied on a system of constant improvement within the firm. Management seeks the feedback of its workers to improve the quality of its vehicles and the efficiency of its design and manufacturing processes. And Toyota seeks the feedback of its customers and dealers too.

Incorporating a feedback loop that effectively allows for trial and error in order to make improvements over time is an important feature of a robust and powerful integrity system.

## Thinking Strategically

UNDERSTANDING HOW CRITICAL integrity is to our economic well-being is a big step. Yet the real power of integrity comes from knowing how to create more. Thinking strategically about integrity and designing integrity systems that are self-reinforcing wealth-creating machines is the exciting possibility we have at our fingertips. We can transform whole areas of the economy that function poorly into integrity systems by keeping in mind the DNA of integrity: disclosure, norms, and accountability.

Consider the opportunities in the nation's dysfunctional health care system. In the current employee-based health insurance system, no one has an interest in doing the right thing. The insured spend money unnecessarily when they know insurance will cover it; doctors may order unnecessary tests if they know insurance will pay; and insurance firms haphazardly apply rules about what they will or will not cover and often change their rules to suit themselves. There's little disclosure from the medical profession or from insurance firms. The public often doesn't understand what doctors, medical services, and medications cost before they agree to pay. The rules governing policies are complex and differ from one policy to the next. And the entire system is set up to perpetuate short-term cheating opportunities.

If done well, investing in integrity can help create a culture of integrity, one in which sound principles are internalized and passed on from one generation to the next, where people have confidence that cheating doesn't pay and instead are encouraged to do the right thing because they understand the financial benefits that creates for everyone.

It's precisely at the moment when our financial and economic problems seem the greatest that we have the chance to improve our system. After all, some of the most significant changes were made when our economic system seemed broken and needed to be rebuilt. During the Great Depression, several brilliant integrity-enhancing policies were designed and implemented that have benefited Americans for decades. The mandated disclosure system of securities law and the FDIC are two examples. Investing in integrity can lay the foundation for America's prosperity for years to come.

## CHAPTER TEN

# The Future of Integrity

. . . . . . . . . . . . . . . . . . . . . . . . . . . . . . . . .

There are good reasons to be optimistic about the future of integrity. The Internet has changed everything. The DNA of integrity—disclosure, norms, and accountability—is fundamentally tied to systems for sharing information. And the cost of collecting, storing, and sharing information has been plummeting. As technology advances, we have the power to create wider and deeper trust across our society. And we can establish trust in places where it never existed before. One example is eBay. Amazon.com, craigslist, Facebook, and other even newer initiatives are changing the way we operate, creating new relationships of trust that didn't exist before. Over time, some of those initiatives will also make it easier to track the integrity of individuals and corporations.

Yet at this moment we have an incredible opportunity at hand. The aftermath of a crisis provides a unique occasion to reimagine the details of the financial system and put the economy on a firm footing. Now is an ideal time to make smart investments that will pay off for years to come. Just throwing money at the problem is not a sufficient answer. Nor are attempts to "fix" the financial system so that people won't be able to do bad things. And searching for villains worthy of the guillotine won't grow our wealth either.

The crisis affords an opportunity too great and too rare to get stuck in old patterns, trying to turn the clock back to an imagined past when everything seemed fine. We have a unique chance to make a quantum step forward in integrity and trust, and in so doing create wealth that spreads widely across our society. That's a critical point to appreciate. Successfully investing in the integrity of our financial system should bring a payoff with widely shared benefits, not just a boost for financial operators.

By understanding the true nature of integrity, its DNA, it's possible to guide the next evolutionary step in a positive direction. To succeed, it is vital to focus on the main goal. There are legions of entrenched interests eager to protect their turf. Each one seeks its own advantage through special pleading and sophisticated public relations, at the expense of the overall system. Complex proposals, special exceptions, and vocal naysayers cloak selfish efforts to avoid change and even attempt new grabs at others' wealth.

Applying the DNA of integrity yields a simple, systematic approach to invest in the integrity of our economy and our collective wealth. With it we can create a better, more valuable system that will bring additional wealth and prosperity to every member of our society.

# Financial Reporting

Markets run on information. When they break down it's usually because information hasn't been all that good. That was certainly the case in the panic of 2008. While widespread proliferation of debt set the stage, poor information about complicated financial products and their risks played a devastating role.

In finance there is a natural tendency to hoard information. Players report what is required but understand on some level that all information is valuable. By disguising the risks involved in securitized and derivative products, dealers were able to maintain the illusion that they weren't very risky. That meant they could continue to profit handsomely from selling toxic investments to overly credulous purchasers.

Secrecy allows those in the know to take more of the pie for themselves. Bringing critical information out in the open helps everyone make better decisions. It makes the pie bigger for all.

When you think about it, there isn't usually a very good public policy reason for financial privacy. It can benefit individuals with valuable knowledge, but secrecy rarely benefits the broader public. The lesson of the panic of 2008 is that in our system of finance we've all become codependent. Our fates are inextricably linked together. We need to look afresh at smart ways to open up the system and allow information to flow freely. That, after all, is one of the most important characteristics of a well-functioning free market.

Disclosure also promotes market discipline. It allows investors to cast their votes—meaning money—in a way that sends a clear message to managers about whether they are doing the right thing. When information is released, the market's reaction provides a clear message to those in charge.

If some investors believe that a company's strategy or prospects are weak, its shares will be sold down. But if information is held back, the market is prevented from adjusting in an orderly way. Hence, crises occur. By the time the true state of affairs is understood, it may be too late for management to change course.

A sensible disclosure scheme would require all financial players—banks, funds, insurers, even individuals—holding more than a threshold amount of investments to periodically disclose their positions in a meaningful way. This would allow market participants to gain the information they need to make good decisions. For instance, a hedge fund could decide whether it wants to do business with a certain bank or vice versa. Financial position reporting would bring a degree of market discipline to major financial players.

Essentially, this would mean disclosing in detail what market players own, what they have borrowed, and the details of their contracts. The point here is that players in the financial system should report their positions on a timely and regular basis, say quarterly, for all to see. A significant size cutoff, say $1 billion in assets, would ensure that the administrative burden falls only on substantial players.

## Bring in the Hedge Funds

Bruce Kovner, founder of Caxton Associates, is known for his secrecy. He doesn't speak to the press and rarely talks at conferences. Nor does he or anyone at his firm reveal much if anything to the public. If Kovner did talk, the world of finance would listen intently. That's because with $6 billion under management and no limits on leverage or risk, his hedge fund can move markets.

While it has significant financial power, Caxton does not have to reveal its inner workings to anyone—even its investors. It is not required to hold any assets aside in case of a crisis. Nor are there restrictions on how much risk it can take on. When the firm first opened its doors twenty-five years ago with $4.7 million under management and the freedom to do as it pleased, it was only a threat to Kovner himself. Today, with pension funds and big asset managers as clients, the risk is spread widely to people who have no clue as to their exposure.

Widespread financial reporting would bring in many of the players, like hedge funds, that are currently allowed to operate in the shadowy world outside the scrutiny of regulators. Hedge funds are explicitly tied into the financial system through their funding. This happens at a number of levels. Traditionally a hedge fund manager puts his own money into the fund and finds other wealthy investors to put their money in too. Lately, an increasing number of pension funds, endowments, and other investment institutions have invested in hedge funds in hopes of boosting returns. Then funds go to banks and borrow money on top of what they take in from investors (leverage) and sign derivatives contracts with the possibility of large losses or gains (risk). So it's no longer just a group of private investors that have exposure to hedge funds. The exposure extends to banks, insurers, pension funds, and their customers. And as the financial crisis has proved, the exposure can ultimately extend to taxpayers as well.

It's thought that at least $2 trillion in assets is managed by hedge funds. Using leverage, their investing footprint could easily be several times that amount. That means a significant portion of the financial system operates completely outside of the normal rules. Hedge funds represent an end run around regulations that were built up over many years, in particular as a result of the hard lessons learned from the Great Depression. But when it comes to discussions about improving the norms and transparency of the hedge fund industry, we're often presented with a false choice: regulate the hedge funds out of existence or don't regulate and have no idea what a large part of the financial system is up to.

Of course, disclosing what they do would be highly unpopular with hedge funds. For years they have resisted any type of disclosure requirements, arguing that if they expose their secret methods, everyone else will use them and they won't be able to profit from all their hard work. But here it's worth taking a minute to be skeptical. Hedge funds needn't disclose their proprietary research. It's what they do that counts, not the underlying reasons. The problem is that when things are hidden, you can't tell who is honest and who isn't until it's too late.

Recall that Bernie Madoff's fraud was detected early on

and reported by a competitor who had access to his figures. But without public disclosure, there was no way for independent researchers to check out Madoff's claims. Tragically, it was all too easy for the SEC to ignore a lone voice of warning.

It's not just a matter of detecting frauds, though. There's a widespread benefit from disclosure. If regulators and investors can see the details of positions being accumulated, they can better assess the risks that build up in the system. During the 2008 financial crisis, it would have been possible to calculate the exposure of the entire system to risky bets on rising house prices, for example. That knowledge might have been enough for some to change their strategy and not get caught when the winds shifted. It might well have been sufficient to safely defuse the incipient crisis. It certainly would have aided in fashioning an appropriate response quickly.

## Getting Real with Banks

BANKS ARE AMONG the most highly regulated financial entities around. And yet a lesson from the financial crisis is that bank reporting is inadequate. For all the information banks disclose, we still seem to lack the most basic understanding of their true financial position.

As the 2008 crisis unfolded, Citibank and Bank of America repeatedly claimed they had adequate capital to cover anticipated losses from deteriorating economic conditions. Yet each ended up requiring mountains of capital from the federal government. And still the market was skeptical that they could continue to operate without the government seizing control. How is it possible that we still have so much uncertainty and disagreement surrounding the true state of the nation's leading banks?

Part of the problem is that banks have moved aggressively into more complex financial instruments where risk is hard to quantify. In addition, banks aren't required to reveal many details about their individual loans on the basis of preserving confidential or proprietary information. Therefore it isn't possible to fully understand the assets banks hold and their associated risks.

First, we should reexamine the desirability of having banks enter into certain types of complicated and risky contracts. In recent years derivatives and structured financial products enabled a gigantic end run around the industry's traditional credit standards and leverage limits. Proponents of "financial innovation" might squawk, but their claims about value creation from financial products need to be viewed in the context of what looks to be the biggest loss handed to taxpayers in the country's history. It seems likely that certain types of products and contracts are not appropriate for firms that we depend on to remain solvent.

We also need better standards for assessing risk, especially relating to financial assets. It's not necessary to start from scratch. The Bank for International Financial Settlements has been working in this area for some time. And regulators could publicly disclose information already gathered by bank supervisors that today is confidential.

As part of bank regulation, supervisory authorities examine the nation's eighty-five hundred commercial banks on a regular basis and assign each one a rating. The components of a bank's condition that are assessed include capital adequacy, asset quality, management, earnings, liquidity, and sensitivity to market risk. Bank examiners are given access to confidential information in order to make their assessments. Looking at all that information and analyzing it already involves considerable expense. Finding smart ways to release what the examiners find to the public is certainly possible. Much could be done without releasing sensitive details of individual loan arrangements. Releasing better information in a simple, clear, and relevant format would be in the public interest and the interest of promoting efficient capital markets.

## Disclosure in the OTC Market

DISCLOSING WHAT'S GOING on in the marketplace is another important step. Part of the problem in the 2008 crisis was owing to a lack of disclosure about how complicated new financial products actually traded.

Among all the kaleidoscopic variety of investment options, many are never traded in public. Publicly traded securities listed on exchanges come under rules requiring issuers to make significant disclosures about their business and finances. In addition, the actual trading of securities on public exchanges is publicly reported.

But for products trading in the over-the-counter (OTC) market, there is fairly limited information about what products are trading and at what price. OTC trading in the United States involves trillions of dollars worth of products. Without official data on how big the OTC market is, it's difficult for the marketplace to assess day-to-day variations in these products. By the time a problem or imbalance is apparent, it can easily be too late to avert a crisis.

There are some simple steps that could be taken to improve OTC disclosure. For one, players could be required to regularly disclose OTC trades and prices so that volume and value could be tallied up by authorities and other interested parties. Since much of the OTC market consists of trading in derivatives that can be complicated and poorly understood, shining some light on these products and keeping track of their status would be a good place to start.

Another step would be to make derivatives a separate disclosure item. Firms entering into a derivatives contract would have to disclose the contract itself. We certainly have the technological capability to publish complicated and opaque derivative contracts for the public to see. Over time, the brilliant minds of finance would surely figure out clever ways to analyze the contracts and provide helpful ways to understand what firms have gotten into and the risks they are taking.

## Norms for Risk

WHILE DISCLOSURE BY itself builds integrity and enhances markets, establishing well-thought-out norms takes us even further. With accepted standards to apply, analysts can study the details of company disclosures and provide quick and efficient guidance to the market about what is acceptable and what isn't.

Traditionally, banks and companies have been evaluated based on their leverage ratio, meaning the amount of debt in relation to equity. Banks, for example, are required to maintain a certain amount of capital in the form of equity to support their debts to depositors. That way there is an adequate financial cushion to absorb potential loan losses before a bank becomes unable to repay its depositors. While many nonbanking firms are not strictly limited in the amount of leverage they can undertake, credit rating agencies pore through the details and provide public credit ratings as a measure of risk.

But there are important gaps in the existing system. The financial system has evolved a number of products and firms whose primary purpose is to get around what are seen as stodgy limits on risk.

Hedge funds, for example, can take unlimited risks. Banks typically are limited to leverage of around twelve to one, meaning they have to take in about nine dollars of shareholder cash for every one hundred dollars of deposits. Investment banks raised leverage to thirty or forty to one prior to the 2008 crisis. At those levels it only takes a loss of 3 or 4 percent on the portfolio of investments to bring on insolvency. Yet it is believed that some hedge funds undertook even higher leverage, anecdotally up to a hundred to one.

The purpose of setting standards on risk, then, would be to extend the rules that apply to banks and insurance companies to hedge funds and investment banks too. That way we would set clear standards on what is acceptable and not acceptable risk taking for all major market players.

But leverage isn't the only measure of risk. Derivatives and structured financial products can operate as leverage in disguise. This is the area where regulations were plainly inadequate in 2008. Citibank and AIG looked fine to regulators based on their apparent leverage ratios. But the risks they were taking in the form of derivatives and other nontraditional investments did not show up as leverage, and thus didn't break any rules. When the market turned, and losses began to cut into their equity, it became apparent that the firms were seriously undercapitalized.

Standards on leverage, then, have to be broadened to take into account derivatives and all other risky contracts. This is an important point for commercial banks and insurance companies that managed to evade leverage standards by using complex derivatives. New standards have to be developed to limit risk taking to appropriate levels.

How can we determine the leverage of complex financial instruments? There are various analytical methods, but these can readily fail if the instruments are designed to create unreasonable risks. And as we've recently seen, the creativity of our financial wizards tends to run well ahead of the thoroughness of our regulations. It is worth questioning whether regulated entities have any business holding complex instruments whose risk cannot be adequately assessed. A good rule of thumb would be if we can't readily assess the risk involved, then we shouldn't allow our important financial institutions to invest. For firms on whose solvency our whole economy depends, we simply can't afford to let them run amok.

While there may be a place for firms that want to take huge risks, we should keep them well separated from innocent bystanders. Fund managers that only use their own money can take as much risk as they like, so long as they are up-front about it and their counterparties agree. But when they borrow heavily from banks, or accept funds belonging to people who can't readily afford to lose their investments, they should have to behave in a prudent manner. Hedge funds that want to borrow from banks or accept institutional money, then, would be subject to leverage standards along with everyone else.

## Cui Bono?

A WISE OLD Roman judge always asked "Cui bono," meaning "To whose benefit?" While the financial marketplace has undeniably become more complex over time, the beneficiaries of all that complexity are not at first obvious. As the panic of 2008 unfolded, it became clear that the heads of investment banks didn't fully understand the products they were involved in. And the ratings agencies that were expected to judge the risks plainly failed to do so.

Take the credit default swap market, for instance. Credit default swaps (CDSs) are in effect bets that have to be paid if a particular borrower defaults on its debt. If no default happens, the buyer wasted its money on the CDS and the seller makes a tidy little profit. But if a default happens, the buyer can be in for a huge windfall and the seller a monstrous loss. During the boom years, major financial institutions gorged on CDSs to the tune of $30 trillion. These contracts were so poorly understood and managed that major financial institutions entered into CDS contract deals with other firms that they couldn't reasonably expect to make good on, at least not without a huge government subsidy.

At the outset, it isn't easy to guess who will win and who will lose on a CDS. But the fees for arranging and selling CDS are substantial, and the arranger makes money on day one. While the complexity brings uncertain results to the principals, the people setting up the deals benefit handsomely. They charge high fees, often depending on how complicated the product or the transaction is. The more tailoring, the higher the fee.

But of course it wasn't just the investment banks and their accountants, lawyers, and ratings agencies that benefited. Buyers of the complex instruments had their reasons too. Although somewhat of an oversimplification, customers want complex arrangements for one of two reasons. They are seeking either to minimize their taxable profits or to maximize their near-term reportable profits. It is relatively rare (though admittedly not impossible) that the contracts are entered into on both sides by investors seeking long-term value creation.

Complicated financial instruments can be very helpful in getting around tax or accounting rules. Complexity therefore has an unfortunate tendency to enable and perhaps even promote negative behavior rather than integrity. And of course reforms to both the tax system and the accounting rules are first and foremost integrity issues.

In fact, investing in the integrity of the tax and accounting systems should go hand in hand with needed changes to the financial system. The three elements together could create a powerful quantum leap in integrity that pays off for years to come.

## Eat Your Own Cooking

ONCE DISCLOSURE AND norms are in place, enforcement becomes a natural consequence. In the run-up to the panic of 2008, disclosure was limited and norms were lacking. That made it very difficult to judge whether an individual or a firm was behaving appropriately. Absent well-thought-out rules, it's hard to call anyone to account. New disclosure rules and new standards would require rethinking penalties and the amount of energy that should be put into investigation and enforcement.

But to maximize efficiency, the financial system has to be empowered to impose its own market discipline independent of regulatory authorities. The natural consequence of effective disclosure and well-developed norms is widespread adherence to those norms. But there are other steps to take to promote accountability.

One step would be to require more personal disclosure from money managers. When you fly on an airplane, you know the pilot has just as much at stake as you do in getting to the destination safely. While that in itself doesn't eliminate crashes, it does make it more likely the pilot will do everything he can to arrive safely. Don't we want the people who manage our savings to behave in the same way?

For those charged with the responsibility of investing funds belonging to others, the public ought to have some idea where they are putting their own money. As Warren Buffet once put it, it would be nice to know whether they eat their own cooking. Widespread personal disclosure would allow the public to follow the actions as well as the words of financial managers.

Of course, there are some hedge fund managers who claim to do that already. It can be a selling point with investors. But knowing that individuals who take risks with other people's money put some of their net worth on the line too would create a powerful integrity mechanism.

## Compensation Structures Matter

WHEN MONEY MANAGERS, bankers, and the like perform well, they should be rewarded. Yet compensation structures that reward individuals for short-term wins have been abject failures. The outrageous risks uncovered in the 2008 crisis were direct results of compensation schemes that rewarded the appearance of profits each year, despite the fact that in many cases those profits ultimately proved nonexistent.

Traditionally, money managers have been judged on their quarterly performance and get paid in relation to their yearly performance. That has created problems for some institutions, where big payouts to managers have preceded big setbacks. During the boom years, many managers put in place strategies that directly or indirectly involved significant risks. When the market turned, these positions were not so easy to reverse without big losses. Some managers were paid enormous sums as they reported high returns in earlier years. If fund managers were compensated for their returns over the long term, even after they left, they would be more careful to adopt sustainable investment strategies.

Reward structures tied to annual performance leave a gaping hole of risk for fund investors, and ultimately for the public. Where the fund manager stands to literally make a fortune by betting the farm—someone else's farm—what incentive is there to be appropriately cautious with all that money? The ideal would be to better match the term of compensation with the term of investment. For example, fund managers could voluntarily subject themselves to compensation arrangements whereby they don't get paid bonuses for paper profits, but instead get their bonuses when the profits are actually cashed out to investors.

The principle could be applied more broadly as well. For example, investment bankers could tie their fees to the long-term success of the companies they advise, rather than getting paid when each deal is signed. Rewarding fiduciaries and advisers over the long term and tying rewards to cash profits would align the interests of managers and investors to promote long-term wealth creation.

## The Feedback Loop

INVESTING IN THE integrity of the financial system won't happen overnight. And it won't come from magic bullet solutions expected to solve all problems. Integrity requires diligent cultivation over time to increase. That means there has to be a feedback mechanism so that we can evaluate what is working and what isn't. Ineffective or inefficient practices can be altered or pruned. Effective ones can be propagated and nourished. Over time, disclosure, norms, and accountability can be fine-tuned to meet changing needs and circumstances.

The vehicles for creating this feedback loop are our supervisory institutions—primarily the SEC and the Federal Reserve. These institutions could be charged with responsibility to evaluate the existing stock of integrity and to propose prudent policies to promote its increase. The supervisors could collect data and opinions to identify new trends and issues. The introduction of new standards and the repeal of old ones could be made a regular process, rather than somnolence interrupted by frantic periods of damage control. With something like the eBay bulletin board, the financial community and the public could give immediate feedback about how the system is working. And like a Toyota manufacturing line, bottlenecks and problems could then be analyzed, discussed, and subjected to continual improvements.

It's clear now that the problems related to the panic of 2008 were due in large part to outdated rules governing the financial system. There was no working mechanism to understand and react to the changes that were occurring in finance.

Establishing an effective feedback loop would ensure that the framework of the financial system was constantly up to date and working well. A financial system that is open, with clear standards for how to take part and long-run accountability, is both possible and a goal worth achieving.

**Steps to Investing in the Integrity of the Financial System**

Disclosure                *Publish details of assets, borrowing, and investment contracts for all major market participants*

Norms                     *Establish standards for risk and leverage*

Accountability            *Require managers to put their own wealth at risk. Tie compensation to multiyear performance*

# ACKNOWLEDGMENTS

· · · · · · · · · · · · · · · · · · · · · · · · · · · · ·

As a journalist, I'm used to people returning my calls and willingly providing information for articles. But nothing prepared me for the tremendous generosity I received while writing this book. Many people gave their valuable time and help in different ways. The reporting for this book was done through interviews in person, on the phone, or via e-mail. I would like to thank each and every person who took my calls, patiently answered questions, dug up data, helped with contacts, or offered smart insights. Among the many who helped in some way, I'd like to acknowledge a few who went above and beyond: Rich Byma, Peter Clifford, David Girardin, Jim Griffith, Jeffrey Liker, Brian Lyons, David Meier, Ronnie Phillips, Steve Shuster, Rick Sullivan, and Mark Zandi.

My writing was done at home in New York and at my homes away from home, the New York Society Library and the Amagansett Public Library. The assistance of Neyssa Campbell at home and the gracious and talented library staffs in New York and on the East End was essential.

When the time came to read the first draft of the manuscript, a few brave friends accepted the challenge and provided critical feedback. I'd like to thank Alexandra Bernasek, Tom McGuire, Jonathan Reiss, and Emiliya Mychasuk.

Writing a book is one thing; publishing is quite another. Without my editor Julia Cheiffetz's determination, support, and unfailing belief in the idea, this book would not exist. At times Julia guided me in ways I resisted, but I soon learned that she had a knack for being right and I am tremendously grateful for all of her help. I'm also grateful to Bob Miller and the brilliant and dedicated staff at HarperStudio who supported, encouraged, and edited this book. And my agent, Kate Lee, provided her experience and helpful advice when I needed it most.

I am incredibly lucky to have supportive family and friends. My girls, Lily and Natalie, cheered me on during the entire book process, as did my parents, Miloslav, Tatiana, Laurie, Mary Jo, and Larry. I'm also grateful for the help I received from friends David Lidsky and Carol Vinzant.

In the end, there is one person who has been immensely generous and supportive every step of way: from the birth of the idea to the finished manuscript and beyond. Without my husband's constant and unlimited help, this book would not have been written.

Thank you all!

# SOURCES

· · · · · · · · · · · · · · · · · · · · · · · · · · · · · · ·

CHAPTER ONE

Arrow, Kenneth. "The Economy of Trust." *Religion and Liberty* 16, no. 3 (Summer 2006).

Grynbaum, Michael M., and John Holusha. "Fed Cuts Rate 0.75% and Stocks Swing." *New York Times*, January 22, 2008.

*The Random House Dictionary of the English Language, Unabridged.* 2nd ed. New York: Random House, 1987.

CHAPTER TWO

"2008 Chinese Milk Scandal." *Wikipedia.* http://en.wikipedia.org/wiki/2008_Chinese_milk_scandal.

Giblin, James Cross. *Milk: The Fight for Purity.* New York: Thomas Y. Crowell, 1986.

Grade "A" Pasteurized Milk Ordinance, 2007 rev. U.S. Department of Health and Human Services, Public Health Service, U.S. Food and Drug Administration.

Jing, Gong, and Liu Jingjing. "Spilling the Blame for China's Milk Crisis." *English Caijing*, October 10, 2008. http://english.caijing.com.cn/2008-10-10/110019183.html.

Ramzy, Austin. "China's Tainted-Milk Scandal Spreads." Time.com, September 26, 2008. http://www.time.com/time/world/article/ 0,8599,1844750,00.html?xid=feed-cnn-topics.

U.S. Food and Drug Administration, Center for Food Safety and Applied Nutrition. http://www.fda.gov.

Wegman, Myron E. "Infant Mortality in the 20th Century, Dramatic but Uneven Progress." *Journal of Nutrition* 131 (2001): 401S–408S.


CHAPTER THREE

The Board of Governors of the Federal Reserve System. http://www .federalreserve.gov.

Friedman, Milton, and Anna Schwartz. *The Monetary History of the United States: 1867 to 1960.* Princeton, NJ: Princeton University Press, 1963.

Hammond, Bray. *Banks and Politics in America: From the Revolution to the Civil War.* Princeton, NJ: Princeton University Press, 1957.

Hayashi, Fumiko, Richard Sullivan, and Stuart E. Weiner. *A Guide to the ATM and Debit Card Industry.* Kansas City, MO: Federal Reserve Bank of Kansas City, 2003.

Mayer, Martin. *The Bankers.* New York: Weybright and Talley, 1974.

NACHA (The Electronic Payments Association). "What is ACH?" NACHA. http://www.nacha.org/About/what_is_ach_.htm.


CHAPTER FOUR

Federal Reserve Bank of New York. "The Key to the Gold Vault." New York: Federal Reserve Bank of New York, 2006.

———. http://www.newyorkfed.org.

## CHAPTER FIVE

Gertner, Jon. "From 0 to 60 to World Domination." *New York Times,* February 18, 2007.

Kotler, Philip, and Gary Armstrong. *Principles of Marketing.* 11th ed. Upper Saddle River, NJ: Pearson Education, 2006.

Lean Associates. http://www.leanassociates.com.

Liker, Jeffrey K. *The Toyota Way.* New York: McGraw-Hill, 2004.

Spear, Steven J. *Chasing the Rabbit.* New York: McGraw-Hill, 2009.

Womack, James P., Daniel T. Jones, and Daniel Roos. *The Machine That Changed the World.* New York: Free Press, 1990.

## CHAPTER SIX

Consumer Reports. "Returns: Prepare to Be Challenged." *Consumer Reports* (December 2006). http://www.consumerreports.org/cro/money/shopping/shopping-tips/holiday-returns-1205/overview.

Kim, J., M. Natter, and M. Spann. "Pay What You Want: A New Participative Pricing Mechanism." *Journal of Marketing* 73, no. 1 (January 2009).

Langendorf, Daniel. "Comedian Hofstetter Experiments with Pay-What-You-Want—and Provides Numbers." last100.com, December 14, 2007. http://www.last100.com/2007/12/14/comedian-hofstetter-experiments-with-pay-what-you-want-and-provides-numbers.

L.L.Bean Company History. L.L.Bean.com. http://www.llbean.com/customerService/aboutLLBean/background.html?nav=ln.

Lynn, William Michael. "Tipping in Restaurants and Around the Globe: An Interdisciplinary Review." In *Handbook of Contemporary Behavioral Economics,* edited by Morris Altman. Armonk, NY: M. E. Sharpe, 2006.

"Radiohead." *Wikipedia.* http://en.wikipedia.org/wiki/Radiohead.

## CHAPTER SEVEN

Anderson, Jenny, and Vikas Bajaj. "A Wall Street Domino Theory." *New York Times,* March 15, 2008.

Geddes, Ross. *IPOs and Equity Offerings.* Oxford: Butterworth-Heinemann, 2003.

Moscrip, Lara. "Mutual Fund Assets Fall Nearly 3% in November." CNNMoney.com, December 30, 2008. http://money.cnn.com/2008/12/30/pf/funds/mutual_funds/index.htm.

## CHAPTER EIGHT

Cohen, Adam. *The Perfect Store: Inside eBay.* London: Piatkus, 2002.

Grameen Foundation. "The Grameen Bank." Grameenfoundation.org. http://www.grameenfoundation.org.

NYSE. The History of the New York Stock Exchange. NYSE.com. http://www.nyse.com/about/history/1089312755484.html.

Stone, Brad. "Former Chief of eBay Tries a New Political Bid." *New York Times,* February 22, 2009.

## CHAPTER NINE

Edwards, Chris. "Cut Taxes, but Simplify Them Too." Cato Institute, May 17, 2001. http://www.cato.org/pub_display.php?pub_id=4202.

Encyclopedia Britannica. "The South Sea Bubble." *Encyclopedia Britannica.* 11th ed. New York: Encyclopedia Britannica, 1911.

Federal Bureau of Investigation. "Uniform Crime Reports." http://www.fbi.gov/ucr/ucr.htm.

Lenter, David, Joel Slemrod, and Douglas Shackelford. "Public Disclosure of Corporate Tax Return Information: Accounting, Economics, and Legal Perspectives." *National Tax Journal* (December 2003).

McChesney, Charles. "Taxpayers Flock to Paid Preparers, Computer Aids." *CNY Business Journal* (March 18, 2005). http://findarticles.com/p/articles/mi_qa3718/is_200503/ai_n13591334.

Mothers Against Drunk Driving. "Campaign to Eliminate Drunk Driving, Statistics." Madd.org. http://www.madd.org/Drunk-Driving/drunk-Driving/Statistics/AllStats.aspx.

Internal Revenue Service. Tax Statistics. Internal Revenue Service. http://www.irs.gov/taxstats.

United Nations Road Safety Collaboration. "Drinking and Driving—An International Good Practice Manual." http://www.who.int/roadsafety/projects/manuals/alcohol/en.

U.S. Securities and Exchange Commission. "The Laws That Govern the Securities Industry." http://www.sec.gov/about/laws.shtml.

CHAPTER TEN

"Bruce Kovner." *Wikipedia*. http://en.wikipedia.org/wiki/Bruce_Kovner.

Caxton Associates Web site. http://www.caxton.com.

Fabrikant, Geraldine. "Harvard Endowment Chief Is Earning Degree in Crisis Management." *New York Times*, February 21, 2009.

Hoenig, Thomas M. "Should More Supervisory Information Be Publicly Disclosed?" Kansas City: Federal Reserve Bank of Kansas City, May 8, 2003.

Jordan, John S., Joe Peek, and Eric S. Rosengren. "The Impact of Greater Bank Disclosure During a Banking Crisis." Boston: Federal Reserve Bank of Boston, February 9, 1999.

Story, Louise. "Hedge Fund Managers to Testify in Washington." *New York Times*, November 12, 2008.

# ABOUT THE AUTHOR

Harry DiOrio © 2009

Anna Bernasek's writing on finance and the economy has appeared in the *New York Times*, the *Washington Post*, the *International Herald Tribune*, *Fortune*, *Time*, and Australia's *Sydney Morning Herald*. She has been a guest commentator on economics on CNN, CNBC, public television, and National Public Radio. Bernasek divides her time between New York City and the east end of Long Island.